GRAMMAR
WORKBOOK
SAT®

ADVANCED
PRACTICE
SERIES

FRIENDS
of the
Davenport Public Library

"Celebrate The Printed Word"
Endowment Fund
provided funds for the
purchase of this item

LEX
Educational Publishers

Created by
Arianna Astuni, President IES
Khalid Khashoggi, CEO IES

Editorial
Christopher Carbonell, Executive Editor
Caitlin Hoynes-O'Connor, Editor
Patrick Kennedy, Editor

Design
Kim Brown, Creative Director
Ana Grigoriu, Book Cover Designer

Authors
Arianna Astuni
Christopher Carbonell
Caitlin Hoynes-O'Connor
Patrick Kennedy
Rajvi Patel

Published by ILEX Publications
24 Wernik Place
Metuchen, NJ 08840
www.ILEXpublications.com
© ILEX Publications, 2014

ON BEHALF OF
Integrated Educational Services, Inc.
355 Main Street
Metuchen, NJ 08840
www.ies2400.com

We would like to thank the ILEX Publications team as well as the teachers and students at IES2400 who have contributed to the creation of this book. We would also like to thank our Chief Marketing Officer, Sonia Choi, for her invaluable input.

The SAT is a registered trademark of the College Board, which was not involved in the production of, and does not endorse, this product.

ISBN: 978-0-9913883-1-8
QUESTIONS OR COMMENTS? Email us at info@ilexpublications.com

TABLE OF CONTENTS

PART I GRAMMAR LESSONS

PART II PRACTICE TESTS

INTRODUCTION

Welcome to the *SAT* *Grammar Workbook* of the *IES Advanced Practice Series.* This specialized workbook is one volume in an SAT preparation series that has been developed by elite SAT teachers at Integrated Educational Services, Inc. (IES). Renowned for its easy, accurate, and efficient SAT techniques, IES has been a leader in the world of SAT preparation. Founded 15 years ago, our company is proud to have contributed to the academic and professional growth of countless students. With its innovative methods, IES is confident that this workbook will be integral to dramatically increasing writing scores.

IES prides itself on delivering comprehensive grammar knowledge that can be understood and applied regardless of a student's personal understanding of the English language. In this IES workbook, the SAT Grammar has been distilled into twelve major types based on recent SAT testing and trends. Over the course of twelve efficient lessons, every SAT Grammar problem will be taught with a clear example followed by an explanation. Our experience has proven that SAT Grammar is best approached by using simplified, clear, and straightforward terms. It is not necessary to be a grammarian or a linguist to ace the SAT Grammar sections. However, it is important to be thorough and knowledgeable of the IES grammar lessons and techniques.

Follow our rules, tips, strategies, and methods to a perfect score!

* SAT is a registered trademark of the College Board, which was not involved in the production of, and does not endorse, this product.

Dear Student:

Having taught SAT for 15 years, I am pleased and honored to offer you the same guidance and the same techniques that have helped all of my students to achieve their targeted SAT scores. My experience in helping students from different backgrounds and varying skill levels has taught me that grammar is best approached when its conventions are explained simply and directly. Every lesson in this workbook is from the same curriculum that I have used in all of my classrooms and privates.

The mission of my company, Integrated Educational Services, Inc. (IES), is to guide students toward their target SAT scores and facilitate access to their desired colleges. In addition to this workbook, our New Jersey and New York locations offer SAT instruction that includes courses, workshops, and individual tutoring. To familiarize yourself with our additional services and products, please visit ies2400.com, where you can view currently available seminars, student and parent testimonials, publications, and much more.

I stand by the adage that practice is one key component of success. But it is even more crucial to practice with quality material – material that is developed by experts and leaders in SAT instruction, by educators who understand the trends of the College Board and the Educational Testing Service. For years, I and my IES SAT specialists have deconstructed and re-engineered SAT test questions for our curriculum. Now, we offer that expertise to you: this book is an arsenal of knowledge that will enable you to succeed on the SAT and open the doors to higher education.

I wish you the best of luck in all of your academic endeavors!

Sincerely,

Arianna Astuni
President, IES

HOW TO USE THIS WORKBOOK

Our lessons are structured around the three **E's**: **E**xample, **E**xplanation, and **E**xercise. Following these "E drills" will prepare you for every grammar problem on the SAT. You will learn visual clues that indicate the specific grammar type being tested in a particular question. You will no longer need to plug in each answer choice until you find the right one. Instead, you will learn to eliminate wrong answer choices quickly and accurately by using the knowledge that this workbook contains.

To master the SAT Grammar, you must know *what* you are being tested on and *how* to notice it. You must break old grammar habits that come from the use of colloquial speech and everyday slang. You cannot rely on how a sentence "sounds." On the SAT, you must apply the rules of grammar that we have collected and clarified in the twelve lessons that follow. With this workbook, you will learn the difference between a "style" change (changing the answer to a random word you "like" better) and a grammatical change (improving the sentence, identifying the sentence error, or improving the paragraph using the laws of grammar).

Most of all, you can use these twelve lessons to effectively identify your weak areas. Then, practice, practice, practice until you reach your target score.

Included

- 12 Essential Grammar Rules Made Easy
- Over 150 Practice Exercises
- 500 Multiple Choice Grammar Questions
- 20 SAT Grammar Sections

Key

 Pay attention to anything with this graphic. Information accompanied by this pencil is crucial to understanding this book's techniques.

 These tips are provided to give you additional knowledge of essential SAT Grammar.

TRY ALL OF OUR ADVANCED PRACTICE SERIES BOOKS

If you like this easy-to-use workbook, check out our other great volumes. The *SAT Grammar Workbook* is part of the *IES Advanced Practice Series* which currently includes a *Reading Comprehension Workbook*, a *Math Workbook*, and the soon to be released *New 2016 SAT Workbook*. Please visit www.ILEXpublications.com to order or find our complete line of SAT workbooks on Amazon.com.

PART I
GRAMMAR LESSONS

Chapter 1
SUBJECT/VERB AGREEMENT

SUBJECT/VERB AGREEMENT LESSON 1

SUBJECT:	The noun or pronoun that indicates what the sentence is about
VERB:	The action of the noun or pronoun
REMEMBER:	Subject/verb agreement is commonly tested by using: is/are, was/were, and has/have. If these words are underlined, check for subject/verb agreement.
AGREEMENT:	All **subjects** and <u>verbs</u> must agree in number.

WHEN YOU SEE a verb underlined, you must ask yourself:

"Who (or what) is doing the verb, and do both subject and verb agree in number?"

SINGULAR	PLURAL
The **girl** <u>jumps</u>.	The **girls** <u>jump</u>.
He <u>is</u> happy.	**They** <u>are</u> happy.

LESSON 1.1

PREPOSITION: Any word (in, at, of, for, to, over, among, between, under…) that indicates a relationship between a noun and another part of the sentence

PREPOSITIONAL PHRASE: Any phrase (in the house, at the mall, to the store, for a jog, under the table…) that begins with a preposition and ends before the verb

Eliminate all PREPOSITIONAL PHRASES. The subject will never be in a prepositional phrase. Prepositional phrases contain extra details that often mislead the reader. CROSSING THEM OUT makes it easier to identify the subject.

EXAMPLE

The cars *in the lot* are clean.

The cars ~~in the lot~~ are clean. → Cross out "in the lot"

The ***cars are*** clean. ✓

One *of the girls* is visiting.

One ~~of the girls~~ is visiting. → Cross out "of the girls"

One is visiting. ✓

LESSON 1.2   **INTERRUPTER:** Any detail positioned between two commas

Eliminate all INTERRUPTERS. The subject will never be in an interrupter. Interrupters contain extra details that often mislead the reader. CROSSING THEM OUT makes it easier to identify the subject.

EXAMPLE

Patrick, *in addition to Tom and Mark*, is coming to the reception.

Patrick, ~~in addition to Tom and Mark~~, is coming to the reception. → Cross out "in addition to Tom and Mark,"

Patrick is coming to the reception. ✓

LESSON 1.3   **TRICKY SINGULAR:** A singular word that sounds plural or is commonly misused as a plural

 Look out for TRICKY SINGULARS (neither, either, everyone, everybody, someone, somebody, anybody, anything, each, anyone, no one, everything, little, and much).

EXAMPLE

Neither of the twins *is* sick.

Neither ~~of the twins~~ *is* sick. → Cross out "of the twins"

Neither is sick. ✓

Either of the rooms at the hotel *is* available.

Either ~~of the rooms at the hotel~~ *is* available. → Cross out "of the rooms at the hotel"

Either is available. ✓

LESSON 1.4   **TRICKY PLURAL:** A plural word that sounds singular or is commonly misused as a singular

 Look out for TRICKY PLURALS (Plural/Singular: data/datum, phenomena/phenomenon, media/medium, and criteria/criterion).

EXAMPLE

The *data* from the computer *are* on my disc.

The *data* ~~from the computer~~ *are* on my disc. → Cross out "from the computer"

The **data are** on my disc. ✓

The *criteria* for the assigned essay *are* very complex.

The *criteria* ~~for the assigned essay~~ *are* very complex. → Cross out "for the assigned essay"

The **criteria are** very complex. ✓

LESSON 1.5   **NEITHER/NOR AND EITHER/OR:** Two subjects separated by a standard phrase

Look out for **NEITHER/NOR** and **EITHER/OR** phrases. Although **NEITHER** and **EITHER** are singular, when grouped with **NOR/OR**, the word that ends the phrase determines the verb.

FORMULA:

Either A or B → B determines the verb   Neither A nor B → B determines the verb

EXAMPLE

Either John or *Mary is* right. ✓   Neither John nor *the Parkers are* wrong. ✓

Sometimes the "B Phrase" includes a prepositional phrase. Apply the technique:

Either the Smiths or *one of the Johnsons was* expected to bring the salad.
Either the Smiths or *one* ~~of the Johnsons~~ *was* expected to bring the salad. → Cross out "of the Johnsons"
Either the Smiths or ***one was*** expected to bring the salad. ✓

LESSON 1.6   **INVERTED SENTENCE:** The verb comes before the subject in a sentence

Look out for anything **INVERTED (VERB/SUBJECT)**. Sentences that start with the word "there" and compound sentences that have more than one subject/verb combination tend to be inverted.

HOW TO CHECK THE VERB:
Simply un-invert (flip) the subject and verb.

EXAMPLE

There <u>is</u> a **cat** in the house.

FLIPPED: *cat is* ✓

During the day, there <u>is</u> **ten cats** in the garage.

FLIPPED: *ten cats is* ✗

ten cats are ✓

When subject nouns are LINKED with an "AND," the subject is PLURAL.

✓   <u>The house</u> **and** <u>the car</u> *were* ruined by the storm.

✓   <u>John</u> **and** <u>Mary</u> *eat* chocolate all day.

✓   <u>The dog</u> **and** <u>the cat</u> *are* in trouble for eating the cake on the counter.

Use this page for additional notes. The following pages have exercises regarding Subject/Verb Agreement.

EXERCISE ONE

DIRECTIONS: Using the strategies you learned on pages 12 - 14, fix the verb(s) where necessary.

EXAMPLE:

is

Neither of the twins ~~are~~ happy about the convention being canceled.

1. By Anita's estimate, there is at least a hundred birds in the tropical rain forest exhibit.

2. There has always been too many conflicting clauses and stipulations in the company's hiring policy.

3. There is a public park, a swimming pool, and a miniature golf course just down the road from the house where I grew up.

4. The principles of morality, government, and perception was all investigated by British philosopher John Locke.

5. Neither Mr. Carruthers nor his son were invited to this year's golf outing.

6. Neither of the contestants were willing to use dishonest methods and thus risk her reputation.

7. The overwhelming support of both emerging and established authors have undeniably enriched the world literature scene.

8. The proceeds from the auction of Ms. Dutton's estate was distributed among her children.

9. Neither the cheerleaders nor the football players themselves believes that the coach has had a positive influence on the team.

10. Either a German novel or a French novel are going to be assigned to the class for summer reading.

11. There is only five more miles to go until we reach our destination.

12. Weather phenomena, from deadly tornadoes to gentle spring rain, is analyzed in great detail on an informative new television show.

13. The building inspectors were astonished to discover that there was three hidden rooms in the basement of the old mansion.

14. Every tenured faculty member of the department of literature and languages were present at Dr. McNulty's retirement party.

EXERCISE TWO

These are examples of questions that you will see on the SAT concerning Subject/Verb Agreement. Follow the directions below.

IMPROVING SENTENCES

Choose the answer that best improves the sentence.

1. The results of using tobacco products <u>is being shown as deleterious to</u> just about all modern studies.

   (A) is being shown as deleterious to
   (B) is shown to be deleterious in
   (C) has been shown as deleterious on
   (D) are shown to be deleterious in
   (E) being deleterious is shown in

2. During medieval times, a new approach to building castles and cathedrals <u>were adopted because of Queen Isabella's influence on</u> England.

   (A) were adopted because of Queen Isabella's influence on
   (B) were adopted by Queen Isabella while influencing
   (C) was adopted due to Queen Isabella's influence on
   (D) was adopted after Queen Isabella's influencing on
   (E) is adopted during Queen Isabella's influence in

IDENTIFYING SENTENCE ERRORS

Choose the answer that correctly identifies the error.

3. <u>There is</u> pencils and calculators <u>at the testing</u>
      A   B
   <u>center already,</u> so there is <u>no need</u> to bring your
      C   D
   own. <u>No error</u>
         E

4. The <u>dilapidated</u> industrial center <u>behind</u> the
         A   B
   cemetery and the <u>run-down housing</u> complex
                     C
   near Main Street <u>has been</u> marked for
                 D
   demolition. <u>No error</u>
          E

(ANSWERS ON NEXT PAGE)

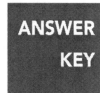

ANSWER KEY — SUBJECT/VERB AGREEMENT

LESSON 1

EXERCISE 1:

1. By Anita's estimate, there *are* at least a hundred *birds* in the tropical rain forest exhibit. **(inverted)**

2. There *have* always been too many conflicting *clauses and stipulations* in the company's hiring policy. **(inverted)**

3. There *are* a *public park, a swimming pool, and a miniature golf course* just down the road from the house where I grew up. **(inverted)**

4. The *principles* of morality, government, and perception *were* all investigated by British philosopher John Locke. **(prepositional phrase)**

5. Neither Mr. Carruthers nor his *son was* invited to this year's golf outing. **(neither/nor)**

6. *Neither* of the contestants *was* willing to use dishonest methods and thus risk her reputation. **(tricky singular/ prepositional phrase)**

7. The overwhelming *support* of both emerging and established authors *has* undeniably enriched the world literature scene. **(prepositional phrase)**

8. The *proceeds* from the auction of Ms. Dutton's estate *were* distributed among her children. **(prepositional phrase)**

9. Neither the cheerleaders nor the *football players* themselves *believe* that the coach has had a positive influence on the team. **(neither/nor)**

10. Either a German novel or a French *novel is* going to be assigned to the class for summer reading. **(either/or)**

11. There *are* only five more *miles* to go until we reach our destination. **(inverted)**

12. Weather *phenomena,* from deadly tornadoes to gentle spring rain, *are* analyzed in great detail on an informative new television show. **(interrupter/tricky plural)**

13. The building inspectors were astonished to discover that there *were* three hidden *rooms* in the basement of the old mansion. **(inverted)**

14. Every tenured faculty *member* of the department of literature and languages *was* present at Dr. McNulty's retirement party. **(prepositional phrase)**

EXERCISE 2:

1. D

2. C

3. A

4. D

Chapter 2
PARALLELISM

PARALLELISM LESSON 2

Making a sentence parallel simply involves making the sentence balanced. Grammar is based on parallel structure.

THE LAWS OF PARALLELISM demand that words or phrases be in the same form of speech (adjectives, verbs, nouns) and use the same structure. Often, balancing a phrase requires the removal of extraneous words.

WHEN YOU SEE lists, comparisons, standard phrases, pronouns, and conjunctions, CHECK for parallelism.

comparisons:	more than, as much as, is, like
standard phrases:	not only/but also, so/that, either/or, neither/nor, prefer/to
pronouns:	one, you
conjunctions:	and, but

LESSON 2.1

EXAMPLE

BALANCING LISTS

She went swimming, running, and danced all night. ✗

She went swimming, running, and **dancing** all night. ✓

This is a call for all professors, editors, and people who collaborate. ✗

This is a call for all professors, editors, and **collaborators**. ✓

LESSON 2.2

EXAMPLE

BALANCING COMPARISONS

Jefferson actually liked to participate in the science league more than he liked playing basketball. ✗

Jefferson actually liked **participating** in the science league more than he liked **playing** basketball. ✓

Jefferson actually liked **to participate** in the science league more than he liked **to play** basketball. ✓

LESSON 2.3

EXAMPLE

BALANCING TWO SIDES OF A STANDARD PHRASE

Judging by the look on his face, Paul is either nervous or filled with excitement. ✗

Judging by the look on his face, Paul is either nervous or **excited**. ✓

I prefer eating salty foods to sweet foods. ✗

I prefer eating salty foods to **eating** sweet foods. ✓

LESSON 2.4	BALANCING PRONOUNS
EXAMPLE	

One should always do what you want. ✗

One should always do what **one** wants. ✓

You should always do what **you** want. ✓

LESSON 2.5	BALANCING TWO SIDES OF A CONJUNCTION
EXAMPLE	

To prepare for the party, we should set the table and making the pasta. ✗

To prepare for the party, we should set the table and **make** the pasta. ✓

John's book is informative but full of entertainment. ✗

John's book is informative but **entertaining**. ✓

As mentioned before, sometimes balancing a sentence merely requires the OMISSION of extraneous words.

✗   The students were happy to learn the lesson, finish the homework and *they could* enjoy the weekend.

✓   The students were happy to learn the lesson, finish the homework, and enjoy the weekend.

Use this space for additional notes. The following pages have exercises regarding Parallelism.

EXERCISE ONE

DIRECTIONS: Using the strategies you learned on pages 20 - 21, balance the sentence if necessary.

EXAMPLE:

Loving
To ~~love~~ is essential, but so is working on your career.

1. In preparation for the train heist, the outlaws obtained ropes and ladders, disguised themselves in black clothing, and they also devised a foolproof escape plan.

2. If you are interested in learning about Italian cinema, one should watch the film *La Strada.*

3. The ballerina was neither committed to a single performance style nor was she willing to ally herself with only one dance troupe.

4. Many students would agree that actually traveling the world is more exciting than when you simply read about faraway places.

5. In recent times, some investment bankers have been more interested in amassing wealth than in how scrupulous the business practices they follow are.

6. To say that Meredith works out "now and then" is underestimating her devotion to health and fitness.

7. Norman yearned not only to write innovative poetry, but also he yearned to create experimental sculptures and architectural designs.

8. Walking through the old haunted house was like a return to all my childhood fears.

9. The Caribbean heritage festival attracted traditional dancers, community service organizers, and documentaries by directors from around the world.

10. Richard is worried not only about how his teachers perceive him, but also about his peers reacting to his personality.

11. Delilah prefers the music of the Rolling Stones to the music which was made by the Beatles.

12. Visitors discovered that the performance art exhibit was not only innovative, but also it educated.

13. My uncle purchased steaks and sausage links, set up his new deck furniture, and he also sent out invitations for his Friday cookout.

14. Compared to its competitors, the new bistro is more spacious and it is more efficiently managed.

15. Linda is neither comfortable speaking in front of others nor is she capable of making her points succinctly.

EXERCISE TWO

These are examples of questions that you will see on the SAT concerning Parallelism. Follow the directions below.

IMPROVING SENTENCES
Choose the answer that best improves the sentence.

1. The car was junked not only because of its unsightly dents <u>but also because its engine was failing</u>.

   (A) but also because its engine was failing
   (B) and also because of the failing engine
   (C) but it also had a failing engine
   (D) but also its engine was failing
   (E) but also because of its failing engine

2. There are many misconceptions surrounding <u>pit bulls and the truth is that they are both loyal and they can be trained easily</u>.

   (A) pit bulls and the truth is that they are both loyal and they can be trained easily
   (B) pit bulls; however, the truth is that they are both loyal and easy to train
   (C) pit bulls, for example, they have both loyalty and can be easily trained
   (D) pit bulls; whereas in truth, they are both loyal and you can train them easily
   (E) pit bulls, they are in truth, both loyal yet easy to train

IDENTIFYING SENTENCE ERRORS
Choose the answer that correctly identifies the error.

3. Jurors need <u>to possess</u> a combination of acumen
   　　　　　　 A
   and <u>be impartial</u> in order to <u>come up with</u> a
   　　　　 B　　　　　　　　　 C
   <u>fair verdict</u>.　<u>No error</u>
   　 D　　　　 E

4. Most people are unaware that all diamonds <u>are</u>
   　　　　　　　　　　　　　　　　　　　　　 A
   rated: <u>a given rating</u> is based <u>on a diamond's</u> carat
   　　　　 B　　　　　　　　　 C
   weight, color, cut, and <u>how clear it is</u>.　<u>No error</u>
   　　　　　　　　　　　 D　　　　　 E

(ANSWERS ON NEXT PAGE)

ANSWER KEY — PARALLELISM
LESSON 2

EXERCISE 1: *THERE ARE MANY WAYS TO CORRECT THE SENTENCES, BUT THE FOLLOWING CORRECTIONS REFLECT SAT STANDARDS.*

1. In preparation for the train heist, the outlaws obtained ropes and ladders, disguised themselves in black clothing, ***and devised*** a foolproof escape plan.

2. If you are interested in learning about Italian cinema, ***you*** should watch the film *La Strada*.

3. The ballerina was neither committed to a single performance style ***nor willing*** to ally herself with only one dance troupe.

4. Many students would agree that actually traveling the world is more exciting than ***simply reading*** about faraway places.

5. In recent times, some investment bankers have been more interested in amassing wealth than in ***following scrupulous business practices.***

6. To say that Meredith works out "now and then" is ***to underestimate*** her devotion to health and fitness.

7. Norman yearned not only to write innovative poetry, ***but also to create*** experimental sculptures and architectural designs.

8. Walking through the old haunted house was like ***returning*** to all my childhood fears.

9. The Caribbean heritage festival attracted traditional dancers, community service organizers, and ***documentary directors*** from around the world.

10. Richard is worried not only about how his teachers perceive him, but also ***about how his peers react*** to his personality.

11. Delilah prefers the music of the Rolling Stones to ***the music of*** the Beatles.

12. Visitors discovered that the performance art exhibit was not only innovative, ***but also educational***.

13. My uncle purchased steaks and sausage links, set up his new deck furniture, ***and sent out*** invitations for his Friday cookout.

14. Compared to its competitors, the new bistro is more spacious and ***more efficiently managed***.

15. Linda is neither comfortable speaking in front of others ***nor capable*** of making her points succinctly.

EXERCISE 2:

1. E
2. B
3. B
4. D

Chapter 3
COMPARISON

Comparison

COMPARISON LESSON 3

Comparison problems are often tricky to catch because the reader infers the correct comparison. Checking for comparison requires the use of visual parallelism. Be aware of what is being compared in the sentence. These comparisons must be LOGICAL.

COMPARISONS	**as, than, like, to, between, among**
"A" PHRASE	**a student, a player, a musician**
WORDS THAT DESCRIBE QUANTITY	**fewer/ less, number/ amount, many/ much**

WHEN YOU SEE these words in a sentence, check for the problems described in the following lessons.

LESSON 3.1	**ILLOGICAL COMPARISONS**

EXAMPLE

In my opinion, there is no story more intriguing than Othello. ✗

EXPLANATION

The word *than* signals that there is a comparison in this sentence. This is not a logical comparison because we must compare a "story" to a "story."

In my opinion, there is no **story** more intriguing than **the story of** Othello. ✓

EXAMPLE

Her inclination to eat a cupcake is much stronger than to go for a jog. ✗

EXPLANATION

This sentence is wrong because her "inclination [to eat a cupcake]" is being compared to "to go for a jog." You must compare *inclination* and *inclination*, not *inclination* and *to go for a jog*.

Her **inclination** to eat a cupcake is much stronger than her **inclination** to go for a jog. ✓

EXAMPLE

Napoleon Bonaparte is more famous than any leader in French history. ✗

EXPLANATION

This sentence is wrong because Napoleon Bonaparte was a leader himself, and he could not have been more famous than himself. We must compare him to *other* leaders.

Napoleon Bonaparte is more famous than any **other** leader in French history. ✓

 When checking for **ILLOGICAL COMPARISON**, think of parallelism: *Pineapples to apples*, **NOT** *pineapples to eating apples*!

LESSON 3.2   **NUMBER AGREEMENT/"A" PHRASE**

 Things that you compare have to agree in *number*. Both are either *singular* or *plural*.

| **EXAMPLE** | Though their parents wished otherwise, they were both struggling to be a musician. ✗ |

| **EXPLANATION** | Because the word "musician" is referring to "they," we must use *musicians*. |

Though their parents wished otherwise, ***they*** were both struggling to be ***musicians***. ✓

| **EXAMPLE** | Both Kristi and Kim are an administrator in the office. ✗ |

| **EXPLANATION** | Because "administrator" is referring to "Kristi and Kim," we must use *administrators*. |

Both ***Kristi and Kim*** are ***administrators*** in the office. ✓

LESSON 3.3   **COUNTABLE/NOT COUNTABLE**

DESCRIBES THINGS THAT ARE **COUNTABLE** (hot dogs, dollars, kisses)	DESCRIBES THINGS THAT ARE **NOT COUNTABLE** (food, money, love)
fewer / number / many	**less / amount / much**

| **EXAMPLE** | There are much more architectural decorations on this skyscraper than I had expected. ✗ |

| **EXPLANATION** | This sentence is wrong because *decorations* can be counted. We must use *many*. |

There are ***many*** more architectural ***decorations*** on this skyscraper than I had expected. ✓

| **EXAMPLE** | No one could guess the number of candy in the jar. ✗ |

| **EXPLANATION** | This sentence is wrong because *candy* cannot be counted. We must use *amount*. |

No one could guess the ***amount*** of ***candy*** in the jar. ✓

LESSON 3.4   **COMPARING EXACTLY TWO VS. THREE OR MORE**

COMPARING ONLY TWO THINGS	COMPARING THREE OR MORE THINGS
between	among
more	most
-er ending words: better, faster, stronger	-est ending words: best, fastest, strongest

EXAMPLE   Of the dozens of kids in the club, Sarah was the more popular. ✗

EXPLANATION   Because there are dozens of kids (3 or more), we must use *most*.

Of the dozens of kids in the club, Sarah was the ***most*** popular. ✓

EXAMPLE   There was no animosity between Joe, Chris, and Patrick. ✗

EXPLANATION   Because there are three people, we must use *among*.

There was no animosity ***among*** Joe, Chris, and Patrick. ✓

When you see BETWEEN or AMONG, remember:

BETWEEN	AMONG
Compares exactly two things Always use "and" Always use "me", not "I"	Compares three things or more Always use "and" Always use "me", not "I"
EXAMPLE The decision is between John or *I*. ✗ The decision is between John ***and me***. ✓	**EXAMPLE** Among Mary, Rhonda or *I*, Mary is the prettiest. ✗ Among Mary, Rhonda ***and me***, Mary is the prettiest. ✓

Use this page for additional notes. The following pages have exercises regarding Comparison.

Comparison

EXERCISE ONE

DIRECTIONS: Using the strategies you learned on pages 26 - 28, fix the comparison error if necessary.

EXAMPLE:

in traveling across

More people are interested in traveling across the United States than ∨ Europe.

1. The ship could not maneuver effectively because too much barrels of provisions and cases of ammunition had been stored on board.

2. In nineteenth-century America, activists such as Elizabeth Cady Stanton and Susan B. Anthony urged women to become a participant in the democratic process.

3. The word problem asked students to determine the amount of marbles that could fill a cylindrical jar.

4. He believes that wearing sandals in summer is better for his health than sneakers.

5. Senator Joseph McCarthy rose to notoriety by determining which citizens of the United States had a communist belief.

6. Terry is firmly convinced that the best comic novels are P.D. Wodehouse.

7. After much deliberation, the judges decided that Grover was the better of the seven performers who had appeared in the talent show.

8. It is hard to deny that flying in a private jet is a much more glamorous way to travel than a commercial plane.

9. Only a few of the air force cadets were interested in becoming an astronaut.

10. Like so many other academic essays on literature, Sharon bombards readers with awkward sentences and unclear definitions.

11. The gardening and yard maintenance duties were equally divided between Jacques, Frederic, and me.

12. Independence and determination are a quality that will lead you to success in your college studies.

EXERCISE TWO

These are examples of questions that you will see on the SAT concerning Comparisons. Follow the directions below.

IMPROVING SENTENCES
Choose the answer that best improves the sentence.

1. What I have experienced while living in Manhattan is drastically different <u>from living in New Jersey</u>.

   (A) from living in New Jersey
   (B) from my experience of New Jersey
   (C) than experiencing living in New Jersey
   (D) than the experience of living in New Jersey
   (E) from what I have experienced while living in New Jersey

2. Philosophy and law are very closely related because <u>they are both a discipline based on intellectual debate</u>.

   (A) they are both a discipline based on intellectual debate
   (B) it is both a discipline, and based on intellectual debate
   (C) they are both disciplines based on intellectual debate
   (D) they are both disciplines based on intellectually debating
   (E) it is both disciplines that are based on intellect and debate

IDENTIFYING SENTENCE ERRORS
Choose the answer that correctly identifies the error.

3. Art and music <u>are</u> some <u>of</u> life's greatest
              A   B
   pleasures <u>but</u> I feel that music is the <u>most</u> accessible.
          C   D
   <u>No error</u>
     E

4. <u>More</u> students attended Lindsay's lectures than
    A
   <u>John</u> because <u>she</u> had flair and a knack for
    B   C
   colorful <u>locutions</u>. <u>No error</u>
          D   E

3

ANSWER KEY — COMPARISON LESSON 3

EXERCISE 1: *THERE ARE MANY WAYS TO CORRECT THE SENTENCES, BUT THE FOLLOWING CORRECTIONS REFLECT SAT STANDARDS.*

1. The ship could not maneuver effectively because too ***many*** barrels of provisions and cases of ammunition had been stored on board.

2. In nineteenth-century America, activists such as Elizabeth Cady Stanton and Susan B. Anthony urged women to become ***participants*** in the democratic process.

3. The word problem asked students to determine the ***number*** of marbles that could fill a cylindrical jar.

4. He believes that wearing sandals in summer is better for his health than ***wearing sneakers***.

5. Senator Joseph McCarthy rose to notoriety by determining which citizens of the United States had ***communist beliefs***.

6. Terry is firmly convinced that the best comic novels are ***those of P.D. Wodehouse***.

7. After much deliberation, the judges decided that Grover was the ***best*** of the seven performers who had appeared in the talent show.

8. It is hard to deny that flying in a private jet is a much more glamorous way to travel than ***flying in a commercial plane***.

9. Only a few of the air force cadets were interested in becoming ***astronauts***.

10. Like so many other academic essays on literature, ***Sharon's essays bombard*** readers with awkward sentences and unclear definitions.

11. The gardening and yard maintenance duties were equally divided ***among*** Jacques, Frederic, and me.

12. Independence and determination are ***qualities*** that will lead you to success in your college studies.

EXERCISE 2:

1. E

2. C

3. D

4. B

Chapter 4
PRONOUN ERRORS (PART I)

PRONOUN ERRORS LESSON 4 (PART I)

SUBJECT/PRONOUN AGREEMENT

PRONOUN: The word that takes the place of the noun

EXAMPLES: I, you, we, us, our, me, he, she, him, her, they, their, it, its

FORMULA: *Janet* is tired because *she* studied for the SAT all day.

WHEN YOU SEE a PRONOUN underlined, you must ask yourself:		SINGULAR	PLURAL
		He/ She, It	They
"Who (or what) is this pronoun referring to and do both (subject and pronoun) agree in number?"		Her/ Him, It	Them
		His/ Her, Its	Their

LESSON 4.1	**DON'T MISTAKE SINGULAR SUBJECTS FOR PLURAL SUBJECTS.**

EXAMPLE	

SUBJECT	PRONOUN
The University of Massachusetts (one place) = the radio station =	IT
people (more than one person) = the doctors = students =	THEY
each of the girls (Tricky Singular) =	SHE
everybody (Tricky Singular) =	HE OR SHE

LESSON 4.2	**JUST LIKE SUBJECT/VERB AGREEMENT, BE AWARE OF TRICKY SINGULARS.**

TRICKY SINGULARS
EITHER, NEITHER, EVERYONE, EVERYBODY, SOMEONE, SOMEBODY, ANYBODY, ANYTHING, EACH, ANYONE, NO ONE, EVERYTHING, LITTLE, MUCH

EXAMPLE	*Everyone* should brush *their* teeth three times a day. ✗
EXPLANATION	*Everyone* is a tricky singular.

Everyone should brush *his* or *her* teeth three times a day. ✓

 Do NOT cross out prepositional phrases. The pronoun's subject may be in the prepositional phrase.

The quality of the *multivitamins* depends entirely on *its* ingredients. ✗

....

What has the ingredients? The quality or the multivitamins?

....

The quality of the ***multivitamins*** depends entirely on ***their*** ingredients. ✓

| LESSON 4.3 | BE AWARE OF TRICKY PRONOUNS. |

 What, where, when, why, who, and *how* are all interrogative pronouns that can begin a question or refer to an unknown. BUT, sometimes they refer directly to the subject.

USE **WHAT** ONLY TO REFER TO A THING.

| EXAMPLE | The quality of the product is **what's** important. ✓ |
| EXPLANATION | *What* refers to quality. Quality is important. |

USE **WHERE** ONLY TO REFER TO A PLACE.

| EXAMPLE | Seattle is **where** I got engaged. ✓ |
| EXPLANATION | *Where* refers to Seattle. I got engaged in Seattle. |

USE **IN WHICH** IF THE "WHERE" IS NOT LITERAL.

EXAMPLE	This is a story where the hero dies. ✗
	This is a story **in which** the hero dies. ✓
EXAMPLE	I like movies where the guy gets the girl. ✗
	I like movies **in which** the guy gets the girl. ✓

USE **WHEN** ONLY TO REFER TO A TIME.

| EXAMPLE | 2014 is **when** the incident happened. ✓ |
| EXPLANATION | *When* refers to 2014. The incident happened in 2014. |

USE **WHY** ONLY TO REFER TO A REASON.

| EXAMPLE | Please tell me **why** you refuse to wear a helmet. ✓ |
| EXPLANATION | *Why* refers to the reason you refuse to wear a helmet. (Please tell me the **reason** you refuse to wear a helmet.) |

USE **WHO** TO REFER TO A PERSON. (Do not use THAT when referring to a person.)

| EXAMPLE | The students that ate got sick. ✗ |
| | The students **who** ate got sick. ✓ |

USE **HOW** ONLY TO REFER TO AN EXPLANATION.

| EXAMPLE | Studying hard is **how** I aced my SAT. ✓ |
| EXPLANATION | *How* refers to studying hard. (I aced my SAT by studying hard.) |

LESSON 4.4   **LOOK OUT FOR AMBIGUOUS PRONOUNS.**

 If the pronoun in the sentence can refer to more than one thing, it is ambiguous. The connection between the subject and the pronoun should be clear.

EXAMPLE   Austin told Joe that *he* had some spinach in his teeth. ✗

EXPLANATION   Who "had spinach in his teeth?" Austin or Joe?

EXAMPLE   Deep-sea exploration has occurred, but *they* still haven't found any new species. ✗

EXPLANATION   Who "haven't found any new species?"

Use this page for additional notes. The following pages have exercises regarding Subject/Pronoun Agreement.

EXERCISE ONE

DIRECTIONS: Using the strategies you learned on pages 34 - 36, fix the pronoun(s) if necessary.

EXAMPLE:

Each year, the local churches collect money to support ~~its~~ *their* charity programs.

1. Everyone that wants a part in the play should report to the auditorium with their script.

2. Although it was over thirty years ago now, I still vividly remember that it was Jacksonville, not Orlando, when I got engaged.

3. Someone forgot their credit card in the lobby of the hotel.

4. The insects, though each distinct in their own way, were all equally despised by Hannah.

5. After a long and contentious deliberation, the soccer association decided that they would punish the offending player by suspending them for two months.

6. Even though the Center for Disease Control has been charged with the task of researching methods to prevent harmful diseases, they often publish findings that are largely ignored by the public.

7. Sometimes, high school students bite off more than they can chew with sports, clubs, and academics.

8. No parent wants to hear that their child is the one that has a bad reputation at school.

9. The Bronx Zoo in New York City is very much concerned with providing their animals with a good quality of life by housing them in habitats that reflects its indigenous environment.

10. Both Lady Gaga and Madonna are known for their stage performances, but she has the more powerful voice.

EXERCISE TWO

These are examples of questions that you will see on the SAT concerning Subject/Pronoun Agreement. Follow the directions below.

IMPROVING SENTENCES
Choose the answer that best improves the sentence.

1. Because of their strong sense of smell, <u>the beagle is often used in an airport to sniff out drugs which are illegal that</u> may be hidden in luggage.

   (A) the beagle is often used in an airport to sniff out drugs which are illegal that
   (B) beagles are often used at airports to sniff out illegal drugs that
   (C) airports often use beagles to sniff out illegal drugs that
   (D) beagles sniff out illegal drugs in airports, that often
   (E) illegal drugs are being sniffed out by beagles that

2. Environmentalists are huge proponents <u>of vehicles that are hybrid cars, which is why they are reportedly very efficient</u>.

   (A) of vehicles that are hybrid cars, which is why they are reportedly very efficient
   (B) of vehicles like hybrid cars, they are reported to be very efficient
   (C) very efficient vehicles because they are reported as hybrid cars
   (D) of hybrid cars as vehicles because they are reportedly very efficient
   (E) of hybrid cars because these vehicles are reportedly very efficient

IDENTIFYING SENTENCE ERRORS
Choose the answer that correctly identifies the error.

3. <u>After watching</u> the romantic comedy <u>that took place</u>
        A   B
   in Ireland, <u>I wanted</u> to visit the city <u>in which</u> the
             C   D
   couple fell in love. <u>No error</u>
                  E

4. <u>Although</u> the university's reputation <u>has suffered</u>
      A   B
   <u>due to</u> the negative attention it has received from
     C
   the media, <u>they are</u> taking strides towards rebuilding
            D
   trust within the community. <u>No error</u>
                    E

(ANSWERS ON NEXT PAGE)

ANSWER KEY | **PRONOUN ERRORS**
LESSON 4 (PART I)

EXERCISE 1:

1. *Everyone who* wants a part in the play should report to the auditorium with *his or her* script.

2. Although it was over thirty years ago now, I still vividly remember that it was *Jacksonville*, not Orlando, *where* I got engaged.

3. *Someone* forgot *his or her* credit card in the lobby of the hotel.

4. The insects, though *each* distinct in *its* own way, were all equally despised by Hannah.

5. After a long and contentious deliberation, *the soccer association* decided that *it* would punish *the offending player* by suspending *him or her* for two months.

6. Even though the *Center for Disease Control* has been charged with the task of researching methods to prevent harmful diseases, *it* often publishes findings that are largely ignored by the public.

7. Sometimes, *high school students* bite off more than *they* can chew with sports, clubs, and academics. *(no error)*

8. No *parent* wants to hear that *his or her child* is the one *who* has a bad reputation at school.

9. *The Bronx Zoo* in New York City is very much concerned with providing *its animals* with a good quality of life by housing them in habitats that reflect *their* indigenous environments.

10. Both *Lady Gaga* and *Madonna* are known for their stage performances, but *she (ambiguous pronoun, must name woman)* has the more powerful voice.

EXERCISE 2:

1. B

2. E

3. D

4. D

Chapter 5

PRONOUN ERRORS (PART II)

PRONOUN ERRORS LESSON 4 (PART II)

WHEN YOU SEE a PRONOUN
you must ask yourself:

"Is this pronoun in the proper form?"

PRONOUN CASE

Similar to SUBJECT/PRONOUN, **PRONOUN CASE** focuses on the correct use of a pronoun in relation to the rest of the sentence. Below are general instances in which the SAT will test PRONOUN CASE.

LESSON 4.5	PEOPLE OR GROUPS

You will see a pronoun combined with ANOTHER PRONOUN, PERSON, or GROUP by a conjunction.

EXAMPLE

The sports team and he…	Sally and they…

Read the following sentence:

Every Sunday at the playground, <u>the other children and her</u> pretended to be valiant knights.

Did you see the problem? If not, here is what you should do when you see a pronoun used in combination with another person or group:

STOP and PLACE YOUR FINGER over the other person or group and REREAD the sentence.

Every Sunday at the playground, ~~the other children and~~ her pretended to be valiant knights.

her pretended ✗	she pretended ✓

Every Sunday at the playground, the other children and **she** pretended to be valiant knights. ✓

EXAMPLE

The school presented the award to Andre and he.

The school presented the award to ~~Andre and~~ he.

presented the award to he ✗

presented the award to *him* ✓

The school presented the award to Andre and **him**. ✓

EXAMPLE

Us and the other parents went to the beach.

Us ~~and the other parents~~ went to the beach.

Us went ✗

We went ✓

We and the other parents went to the beach. ✓

LESSON 4.6   **THAN OR AS**

Pronoun Case may also appear in comparisons usually indicated by the words THAN or AS:

No one did better than <u>her</u>.	No one has scored as many touchdowns as <u>him</u>.

In both sentences, there is an implied verb after the pronoun. Here is what you should do: INSERT the implied verb to REVEAL the correct pronoun.

No one did better than her (did).	No one has scored as many touchdowns as him (scored).
her did ✗	him scored ✗
she did ✓	*he* scored ✓
No one did better than **she**. ✓	No one has scored as many touchdowns as **he**. ✓

EXAMPLE

Betty is faster than me.	Chris is as noisy as her.
Betty is faster than me (am).	Chris is as noisy as her (is).
me am ✗	her is ✗
I am ✓	*she* is ✓
Betty is faster than *I*. ✓	Chris is as noisy as *she*. ✓

LESSON 4.7   **REFLEXIVE PRONOUNS**

Another way that you will see PRONOUN CASE is in REFLEXIVE PRONOUNS such as *himself, herself, themselves, ourselves,* and *myself*. Note: *myself* is the most commonly used on the SAT. If you see *me* or *myself* underlined, check to make sure the pronoun is being used properly.

To celebrate my graduation, I scheduled a party <u>for me</u> and the other graduates.

I scheduled a party for me ✗
I scheduled a party for *myself* ✓

To celebrate my graduation, I scheduled a party for **myself** and the other graduates. ✓

LESSON 4.8   **BETWEEN / AMONG**

Do you recall the tip from comparison about "BETWEEN" and "AMONG"?
Always use "me" not "I". The same rule applies in these cases. When you see
the words *between* and *among* use the **OBJECTIVE** form of the pronoun. See
table below.

SUBJECTIVE	OBJECTIVE
I	Me
He	Him
She	Her
We	Us

EXAMPLE

Between Mary and I ✗	Between Mary and *me* ✓

Among Stacy, Richard and she ✗	Among Stacy, Richard, and her ✓

Use this page for additional notes. The following pages have exercises regarding Pronoun Case.

EXERCISE ONE

DIRECTIONS: Using the strategies you learned on pages 42 - 44, circle the correct pronoun.

(is)

EXAMPLE: I am better at tennis than (her / (she)) and thus, I win every game.

1. Despite our differences, Yolanda and (I / me) must work together on this science project.

2. No one is sorrier than (I / me) that you lost your dog.

3. Gertrude was trying to provoke me the whole night, but I had to remind (me / myself) not to dignify her antics with a response.

4. After the shopping spree, we all agreed that no one had spent more than (she / her).

5. Did Dad bring any exotic souvenirs home for Keshav and (I / me)?

6. (We / Us) and the rest of our posse decided that in order to assert our territory on the beach, we would need to bring a blanket and multiple chairs.

7. The man making the broccoli and cheddar soup accidentally spilled it all over my Yorkshire Terrier and (I / me)

8. (He and I / Him and me) work well together.

9. Even though I wore my best dress and my most dramatic hairdo, none of the boys at the event would dance with (I / me).

10. Over the course of 28 years, Kelly, Linda, and (he / him) cultivated a bountiful pumpkin patch.

11. The other Civil War reenactors and (she / her) got into a dispute with the municipal parks department about the use of real cannons.

12. Since we were provided with a pamphlet about the mating habits of apes, it was easy for (she and I / her and me) to spot indications of romance at the gorilla exhibit.

EXERCISE TWO

These are examples of questions that you will see on the SAT concerning Pronoun Case. Follow the directions below.

IMPROVING SENTENCES
Choose the answer that best improves the sentence.

1. After the basketball game, Carly, Courtney, and <u>me was exhausted and exhilarated so that</u> we couldn't decide if we should go home or go out.

    (A) me was exhausted and exhilarated so that
    (B) me were exhausted and exhilarated so
    (C) I was so exhausted and exhilarated yet
    (D) I were so exhausted yet exhilarated that
    (E) I were exhausted and exhilarated to where

2. While tidying up at home, I realized that <u>no one is as organized as me</u>.

    (A) no one is as organized as me
    (B) no one had been as organized as I
    (C) no one is organizing as me
    (D) no one is as organized than me
    (E) no one is as organized as I

IDENTIFYING SENTENCE ERRORS
Choose the answer that correctly identifies the error.

3. <u>Every day</u> after lunch, a few of my coworkers
      A
and <u>me</u> go for a walk around <u>our</u> campus
      B   C
<u>to keep fit</u>. <u>No error</u>
  D   E

4. Even though <u>there</u> were times when we got under
            A
<u>each other's skin</u>, there is no animosity
        B
<u>between</u> Jay and <u>me</u>. <u>No error</u>
  C   D   E

5

PRONOUN ERRORS

LESSON 4 (PART II)

EXERCISE 1:

1. Despite our differences, Yolanda and *I* must work together on this science project.

2. No one is sorrier than *I* that you lost your dog.

3. Gertrude was trying to provoke me the whole night, but I had to remind *myself* not to dignify her antics with a response.

4. After the shopping spree, we all agreed that no one had spent more than *she*.

5. Did Dad bring any exotic souvenirs home for Keshav and *me*?

6. *We* and the rest of our posse decided that in order to assert our territory on the beach, we would need to bring a blanket and multiple chairs.

7. The man making the broccoli and cheddar soup accidentally spilled it all over my Yorkshire Terrier and *me*.

8. *He and I* work well together.

9. Even though I wore my best dress and my most dramatic hairdo, none of the boys at the event would dance with *me*.

10. Over the course of 28 years, Kelly, Linda, and *he* cultivated a bountiful pumpkin patch.

11. The other Civil War reenactors and *she* got into a dispute with the municipal parks department about the use of real cannons.

12. Since we were provided with a pamphlet about the mating habits of apes, it was easy for *her and me* to spot indications of romance at the gorillas exhibit.

EXERCISE 2:

1. D

2. E

3. B

4. E

Chapter 6

DANGLING MODIFIER

DANGLING MODIFIER LESSON 5

A DANGLING MODIFIER IS A DESCRIPTIVE PHRASE FOLLOWED BY THE WRONG SUBJECT.

MODIFIER:
Descriptive phrase —→ (Regularly lifting heavy packages,) (John) hurt his back. ✓

SUBJECT: The person or other noun that the modifier describes

WHEN YOU SEE a sentence beginning with a modifier... —→ Ask yourself, **WHO** or **WHAT** does this descriptive phrase apply to?

LESSON 5.1	**PLACING THE SUBJECT AFTER THE MODIFIER (THUS AFTER THE COMMA)**
EXAMPLE	Known to be poisonous, the unsuspecting tourist was bitten by the rattlesnake. ✗
EXPLANATION	*Who* is known to be poisonous–the tourist, or the rattlesnake?
	Known to be poisonous, the rattlesnake bit the unsuspecting tourist. ✓
EXAMPLE	Walking down the street, Jane saw a shooting star. ✓
EXPLANATION	If JANE is walking down the street, then JANE must come right after the comma.

LESSON 5.2	**THE APOSTROPHE TRAP**

BE CAREFUL not to pick a subject that is a possessive noun, or a subject with an apostrophe (Picasso's paintings; Carol's legs). The apostrophe means ownership, so the word following it cannot be separated from the person. They must remain together unless the apostrophe is removed.

EXAMPLE	Walking down the street, Jane's head was almost cut off by a shooting star. ✗
EXPLANATION	*Jane's head* was not walking down the street.
EXCEPTION	Pounding like a hammer, Jane's headache would not stop. ✓
EXPLANATION	*Jane's headache* was pounding like a hammer, so there is no dangling modifier.

LESSON 5.3	DANGLING MODIFIERS AT THE END OF THE SENTENCE
EXAMPLE	Raj swallowed his last bite of watermelon parking the truck. ✗
EXPLANATION	*His last bite of watermelon* was not parking the truck.
	Parking the truck, Raj swallowed his last bite of watermelon. ✓

Use this page for additional notes. The following pages have exercises regarding Dangling Modifier.

EXERCISE ONE

DIRECTIONS: Using the strategies you learned on pages 50 - 51, fix the Dangling Modifier if necessary.

EXAMPLE:

While attending college, <u>her family</u> was happy to see <u>Cindy</u> every weekend.

1. Without any formal training, the landscape paintings by Rhonda were beautiful.

2. Famous for having popularized colorful socks, Harry's shoes also have a stylish flair.

3. Before taking off into the sunset, the kiss the cowboy shared with his lover was passionate.

4. The teacher was proud that by lightening the homework load, her students' performance and participation in class increased.

5. Kandi invented a new toilet that cleans itself when pulling a lever.

6. Hoping that her performance had been good enough to earn her a spot in the cheerleading squad, Caroline waited in the hallway.

7. Worn out after years of use, Jacob needed to replace his favorite pair of jeans.

8. Perhaps his finest work, Picasso created a mural-sized painting in black and white called *Guernica*.

9. Easily the most sought-after countertop material, most people want granite for its durability and attractiveness.

10. Having climbed for days, the torrential downpour forced the disheartened travelers to abandon their goal of reaching the summit.

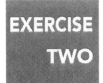

EXERCISE TWO

These are examples of questions that you will see on the SAT concerning Dangling Modifier. Follow the directions below.

IMPROVING SENTENCES
Choose the answer that best improves the sentence.

1. After realizing her car was parked in a distant lot, there was a long walk ahead of Jessica.

   (A) After realizing her car was parked in a distant lot, there was a long walk ahead of Jessica.
   (B) Jessica realized there was a long walk ahead of her, her car was parked in a distant lot.
   (C) There was a long walk ahead of Jessica after realizing her car was parked in a distant lot.
   (D) Parked in a distant lot, Jessica realized there was a long walk ahead of her to the car.
   (E) After realizing her car was parked in a distant lot, Jessica had a long walk ahead of her.

2. Because they are stealthy and hunt at night, only through the use of special night-vision equipment can certain big cats be studied by scientists.

   (A) only through the use of special night-vision equipment can certain big cats be studied by scientists
   (B) certain big cats can only be studied by scientists through the use of special night-vision equipment
   (C) scientists, only through the use of special night-vision equipment, can study certain big cats
   (D) a certain big cat can only be studied by scientists' use of special night-vision equipment.
   (E) certain big cats, through the use of special night-vision equipment, can only be studied by scientists

IDENTIFYING SENTENCE ERRORS
Choose the answer that correctly identifies the error.

3. After searching the whole of Brooklyn, I finally
      A   B
   found the thrift store walking in Williamsburg.
     C   D
   No error
     E

4. As it turns out, these shoes may be too small
       A   B
   because they don't fit when tying the laces.
     C   D
   No error
     E

(ANSWERS ON NEXT PAGE)

ANSWER KEY

DANGLING MODIFIER

LESSON 5

EXERCISE 1: *THERE ARE MANY WAYS TO CORRECT THE SENTENCES, BUT THE FOLLOWING CORRECTIONS REFLECT SAT STANDARDS.*

1. Without any formal training, Rhonda made beautiful landscape paintings.

2. Famous for having popularized colorful socks, Harry also wears shoes with a stylish flair.

3. Before taking off into the sunset, the cowboy shared a passionate kiss with his lover.

4. The teacher was proud that by lightening the homework load, she increased her students' performance and participation in class.

5. Kandi invented a new toilet that cleans itself when its lever is pulled.

6. Hoping that her performance had been good enough to earn her a spot in the cheerleading squad, Caroline waited in the hallway. *(no error)*

7. Worn out after years of use, Jacob's favorite pair of jeans need to be replaced.

8. Perhaps his finest work, Picasso's *Guernica* is a mural-sized painting in black and white.

9. Easily the most sought-after countertop material, granite is wanted for its durability and attractiveness.

10. Having climbed for days, the travelers were disheartened that the torrential downpour forced them to abandon their goal of reaching the summit.

EXERCISE 2:

1. E

2. B

3. D

4. D

Chapter 7

ADJECTIVE VS. ADVERB

ADJECTIVE VS. ADVERB LESSON 6

WHEN YOU SEE a descriptive word UNDERLINED – stop and ask yourself:

"What is it describing? Is it describing a noun, verb, or adjective?"

Lilly is **AMAZING** at baseball.

Madison **SLOWLY** jogged on Sunday.

The movie was **DISTURBINGLY** horrific.

LESSON 6.1   **ADJECTIVE:** The word that describes a noun

EXAMPLE

1. Jane is *beautiful*. Beautiful describes *Jane*.

2. The beat is *constant*. Constant describes *the beat*.

3. She is a *safe* driver. Safe describes *her as a driver*.

LESSON 6.2   **ADVERB:** The word that describes a verb or an adjective

EXAMPLE   **Adverbs describing verbs**

1. Jane runs *beautifully*. Beautifully describes how Jane *runs*.

2. The beat is *constantly* playing. Constantly describes how the beat is *playing*.

3. Drive *safely*. Safely describes how to *drive*.

EXAMPLE   **Adverbs describing adjectives**

1. She is *amazingly* quick. Amazingly describes how *quick* she is.

2. She is *breathtakingly* pretty. Breathtakingly describes how *pretty* she is.

3. The casserole came out of the oven with a *horrifically* burnt top layer. Horrifically describes how *burnt* the top layer was.

ADJECTIVE VS. ADVERB seems like an easy type to detect. But the College Board test makers are very adept at picking adjectives and adverbs that do not sound wrong even when used incorrectly.

Use this page for additional notes. As you complete practice tests, write down the adjectives and adverbs that you find. This can be used for further study. The following pages have exercises regarding Adjective vs. Adverb.

EXERCISE ONE

DIRECTIONS: Using the strategies you learned on page 56, correct the adjective or adverb if needed.

EXAMPLE:

swiftly

The calm river became wild due to the s~~w~~ift changing storm.

1. Although my dentist does a thoroughly job cleaning my teeth, he lacks charisma.

2. Jennifer and Austin were awarded the highest honors in the class for their ingenious science projects.

3. No matter how hard you try, you will never steal the recipe for my moist and sweetly brownies.

4. Whenever he mows the lawn, Akshay sings enthusiastic because nobody can hear him above the roar of the lawnmower.

5. Even though I understand that my comments were offensive, you should cut me a break because I only meant them joking.

6. In today's society, finding affordable and sustainable energy sources is more important than owning irresponsible immense homes.

7. Sravani is our new intern at the office; her acumen and diligence make her a likely candidate for an officially position.

8. Despite the fact that the black bear at my local nature reserve is general harmless, inconsiderate tourists sometimes move this animal to wrath.

9. Maya Angelou, a gifted poet, literary legend, and fervently dancer, died on May 28, 2014, at the ripe old age of 86.

10. Just because you are more skilled at the steel drums than I, you do not have the right to regard me condescendingly.

These are examples of questions that you will see on the SAT concerning Adjective Vs. Adverb. Follow the directions below.

IMPROVING SENTENCES
Choose the answer that best improves the sentence.

1. The advent of smart phones <u>has put undue pressure on our youth to be continuous connected to the Internet, and this pressure</u> has led to a decrease in mental stamina in class.

   (A) has put undue pressure on our youth to be continuous connected to the Internet, and this pressure
   (B) has put undue pressure on our youth to be continuously connected to the Internet, and this pressure
   (C) have put undue pressure on our youth to be continuous connected to the Internet, and this pressure
   (D) has put undue pressure on our youth to be continuously connected to the Internet, this pressure
   (E) have put undue pressure on our youth to be continuously connected to the Internet, and also the pressure

2. The eucalyptus plant, <u>a staple in the diet of the Koala bear, produces oil that serves as a usefully and natural insecticide</u>.

   (A) a staple in the diet of the Koala bear, produces oil that serves as a usefully and natural insecticide
   (B) a staple in the diet of the Koala bear, produce oil that serve as a useful and natural insecticide
   (C) a staple in the diet of the Koala bear, produces oil that serves as a useful and natural insecticide
   (D) a staple in the diet of Koala bears, produce oil that serves as a useful and natural insecticide
   (E) a staple in the diet of the Koala bear, it produces oil that serves as a usefully and natural insecticide

IDENTIFYING SENTENCE ERRORS
Choose the answer that correctly identifies the error.

3. When <u>we</u> visited the Grand Canyon last year, we <u>took</u>
      A   B
   a raft down the Colorado River that, despite <u>its</u> basic
                                           C
   materials, did an <u>adequately</u> job at protecting us from the
                         D
   white water. <u>No error</u>
             E

4. <u>Even though</u> Jasper was lucky <u>to have won</u> the lottery last
       A   B
   year, he <u>foolishly</u> squandered most of his fortune on additional
              C
   lottery tickets, and now has <u>less money</u> than he did before
                              D
   he won. <u>No error</u>
          E

(ANSWERS ON NEXT PAGE)

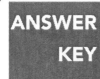

ADJECTIVE VS. ADVERB
LESSON 6

Answer Key

EXERCISE 1:

1. Although my dentist does a *thorough* job cleaning my teeth, he lacks charisma.

2. Jennifer and Austin were awarded the highest honors in the class for their ingenious science projects. *(no error)*

3. No matter how hard you try, you will never steal the recipe for my moist and *sweet* brownies.

4. Whenever he mows the lawn, Akshay sings *enthusiastically* because nobody can hear him above the roar of the lawnmower.

5. Even though I understand that my comments were offensive, you should cut me a break because I only meant them *jokingly*.

6. In today's society, finding affordable and sustainable energy sources is more important than owning *irresponsibly* immense homes.

7. Sravani is our new intern at the office; her acumen and diligence make her a likely candidate for an *official* position.

8. Despite the fact that the black bear at my local nature reserve is *generally* harmless, inconsiderate tourists sometimes move this animal to wrath.

9. Maya Angelou, a gifted poet, literary legend, and *fervent* dancer, died on May 28, 2014, at the ripe old age of 86.

10. Just because you are more skilled at the steel drums than I, you do not have the right to regard me condescendingly. *(no error)*

EXERCISE 2:

1. B

2. C

3. D

4. E

Chapter 8
IRREGULAR VERBS

IRREGULAR VERBS LESSON 7

IRREGULAR VERBS: Verbs that are not conjugated by simply adding an "s" or "ed". Irregular verbs change spelling when tense changes.

WHEN YOU SEE a verb underlined, you must ask yourself:

Is there a "had/have" before it?
Does this verb change spelling when tense changes?

NORMAL VERB	
slap → slapped	step → stepped
→ had slapped	→ had stepped

IRREGULAR VERB	
break → broke	drink → drank
→ had broken	→ had drunk

LESSON 7.1   **IRREGULAR VERBS**

Changing "IRREGULAR VERBS" to past tense or to the "had/have" tenses is not straightforward. An easy way to spot irregular verbs on the SAT is to look for an irregular verb alone or an irregular verb paired with a *had* or *have*.

EXAMPLE

drive → drove	know → knew	creep → crept
→ had/have driven	→ had/have known	→ had/have crept

Anytime there is a **had** or **have** in front of an irregular verb, it changes its spelling to incorporate a **u**, **m**, or **n**. In simplest terms, if you see an irregular verb with a **u**, **m**, or **n** in it, it must have **had** or **have**. See below.

EXAMPLE   By the time Jeffery *had drove* to California, the rocky road ice cream stored in the trunk of his car was completely melted and inedible.

EXPLANATION   The verb *drive* is conjugated to *drove* to indicate past tense. However, because there is a *had* next to it, we must change *drove* to *driven*.

By the time Jeffery **had driven** to California, the rocky road ice cream stored in the trunk of his car was completely melted and inedible. ✓

NOTE: There are some exceptions to the *u, m, n* rule, but they are not tested on the SAT.

WHENEVER YOU SEE "had" or "have" right before a verb, check that the verb is in the correct form. Refer to the list on the next page for an illustration of this principle. This list is not comprehensive, but it will give you a good foundation for checking this type of error in the future.

Irregular Verbs

COMMON IRREGULAR VERBS ON THE SAT

INFINITIVE	PAST TENSE	"HAD" OR "HAS"/"HAVE"
To arise	Arose	Arisen
To awake	Awoke	Awoken
To beat	Beat	Beaten
To begin	Began	Begun
To bite	Bit	Bitten
To blow	Blew	Blown
To break	Broke	Broken
To choose	Chose	Chosen
To do	Did	Done
To draw	Drew	Drawn
To drink	Drank	Drunk
To drive	Drove	Driven
To eat	Ate	Eaten
To freeze	Froze	Frozen
To fly	Flew	Flown
To forsake	Forsook	Forsaken
To forget	Forgot	Forgotten
To go	Went	Gone
To know	Knew	Known
To ride	Rode	Ridden
To run	Ran	Run
To sing	Sang	Sung
To sink	Sank	Sunk
To speak	Spoke	Spoken
To spring	Sprang	Sprung
To swim	Swam	Swum
To take	Took	Taken
To tear	Tore	Torn
To write	Wrote	Written

NOTE the common change in the third column. The verbs now have a *u*, *m*, or *n*. When the helping verb is added, the main verb takes on a new form.

Irregular Verbs

DIRECTIONS: Using the strategies you learned on pages 62 - 63, fix the irregular verb if necessary.

EXAMPLE: *forgotten*

Have we for̶got the necessity of human kindness?

1. I should have knew that Henry was going to betray me: his shifty eyes were a dead giveaway.

2. Mickey told me that you had beat the principal in the student-faculty tennis tournament.

3. Even though the sandcastles that we built last summer have sunk into the ground, my memories of that idyllic vacation will never fade away.

4. I would have wrote the letter if the stationary I wanted to use had been available.

5. Since Ananya is such a kind girl, I did not expect you to have spoke to her in such a nasty tone.

6. Until thirty-five years ago, Sachin had always rode his bicycle to school.

7. If you had froze the steak, it would not have gone bad so soon.

8. The students should have taken the extension that the professor offered them; instead, they insisted on finishing on time with just a mediocre presentation.

9. Janet decided that she needed to go to the bathroom only after the concert had began.

10. In his youth, Kenji, like his other friends, had forsook his former lifestyle to pursue the freedom of living as a vagabond in California.

EXERCISE
TWO

These are examples of questions that you will see on the SAT concerning Irregular Verbs.
Follow the directions below.

IMPROVING SENTENCES
Choose the answer that best improves the sentence.

1. Had I been informed of the weather report, I would
have did more storm preparation, like perhaps
bringing an umbrella.

(A) Had I been informed of the weather report, I
would have did more storm preparation, like
perhaps bringing an umbrella.
(B) If I would have been informed of the weather
report, I would have did more storm
preparation, like perhaps bringing an umbrella.
(C) Had I been informed of the weather report, I
would have done more storm preparation;
perhaps I would have brought an umbrella.
(D) Had I been informed of the weather report, I
would have done more storm preparation, for
example, I would have brought an umbrella.
(E) Had I been informed of the weather report, I would
have done more storm preparation: I would
have brung an umbrella.

2. After Michael failed his physical endurance test, he
realized that he had drank too many chocolate
milkshakes the night before.

(A) test, he realized that he had drank too many
chocolate milkshakes the night before
(B) test, he realized that he had drunk too many
chocolate milkshakes the night before
(C) test; he realized that he had drunk too many
chocolate milkshakes the night before
(D) test, then he realizes how he had drank too many
chocolate milkshakes the night before
(E) test, realizing how he had drunk too many
chocolate milkshakes the night before

IDENTIFYING SENTENCE ERRORS
Choose the answer that correctly identifies the error.

3. If you had spoken wisely before the king as you
         A   B
were commanded to do, maybe you would not have been
                              C
thrown into the dungeon with all the other prisoners.
                                        D
No error
 E

4. By the time Javier was finished preparing the fluffy

pancakes, poached eggs, and crispy bacon, Jessica
                        A
had not only arose, but had also walked down the
            B
three flights of stairs, following the delicious scent of
    C   D
breakfast. No error
              E

EXERCISE 1:

1. I should have *known* that Henry was going to betray me: his shifty eyes were a dead giveaway.

2. Mickey told me that you *had beaten* the principal in the student-tennis tournament.

3. Even though the sandcastles that we built last summer have sunk into the ground, my memories of that idyllic vacation will never fade away. *(no error)*

4. I would have *written* the letter if the stationary I wanted to use had been available.

5. Since Ananya is such a kind girl, I did not expect you to have *spoken* to her in such a nasty tone.

6. Until thirty-five years ago, Sachin had always *ridden* his bicycle to school.

7. If you had *frozen* the steak, it would not have gone bad so soon.

8. The students should have taken the extension that the professor offered them; instead, they insisted on finishing on time with just a mediocre presentation. *(no error)*

9. Janet decided that she needed to go to the bathroom only after the concert had *begun*.

10. In his youth, Kenji, like his other friends, had *forsaken* his former lifestyle to pursue the freedom of living as a vagabond in California.

EXERCISE 2:

1. C

2. B

3. E

4. B

Chapter 9
VERB TENSE

VERB TENSE LESSON 8

There are a multitude of tenses in the English language. It is not necessary for the purpose of the SAT to learn and/or memorize every single tense.

The best way to master verb tense questions is to recognize when you are being tested on tense:

WHEN YOU SEE the following references to time in the sentence, use your basic knowledge of tense to check for an error.

YEARS	1969, nineteenth century
DATES	On October 6th, 1999
TIME	2PM, 15 hours
TENSE WORDS	year, later, after, since, yesterday, tomorrow, ago, past, future

Though the SAT does not test your in-depth knowledge of tenses, it will expect you to know the basic guidelines in this chapter:

LESSON 8.1   **HAS/HAVE**

When you see HAS or HAVE before the verb, it should refer to an action or condition that began in the past, has continued to the present, and perhaps may continue into the future.

EXAMPLE

I went to see the fireworks since I was four years old. ✘

I *have been going* to see fireworks since I was four years old. ✓

LESSON 8.2   **HAD**

When you see HAD before the verb, it should refer to an event or condition that occurred prior to another event in the past.

EXAMPLE

By the time George organized his closet, his mother berated him about his filthy room. ✘

By the time George organized his closet, his mother *had berated* him about his filthy room. ✓

LESSON 8.3   **PAST TENSE (PART 1)**

When the sentence establishes PAST TENSE, verbs describing action should not end in *ing*.

EXAMPLE

Fifty years ago, Isabella marrying a rich banker just for his money. ✘

Fifty years ago, Isabella *married* a rich banker just for his money. ✓

LESSON 8.4 PAST TENSE (PART 2)

If you see an underlined verb and you are unsure if you should change the tense, USE THE CONTEXT of the rest of the sentence to clarify the tense of the verb in question.

EXAMPLE

Megha *arrives* at the train station just when the ticket booth closed. ✗

Megha ***arrived*** at the train station just when the ticket booth closed. ✓

The word "being" is often wrong.

Jonathan *being remembered* because of his valiant efforts during the hurricane rescue and his legacy will endure. ✗

Jonathan ***will be remembered*** because of his valiant efforts during the hurricane rescue and his legacy will endure. ✓

Use this space for additional notes. The following pages have exercises regarding Verb Tense.

EXERCISE ONE

DIRECTIONS: Using the strategies you learned on pages 68 - 69, fix the Verb Tense if necessary.

EXAMPLE:

has continued

Ramona was hired as a director at a small company and ~~was continuing~~ in this capacity ever since.

1. In 1979, the Islamic Republic of Iran being established.

2. Sandy regretted his decision to ignore his parents' curfew: when he gets home late, they were waiting at the door with a list of punishments.

3. After Olga had thrown me out of her apartment, I thought that perhaps I should not have tried to bathe my pet goat in her shower.

4. Fiona was writing her novel for nine hours straight, and she is still going strong.

5. In 1969, the famous Woodstock concert attracting hordes of people.

6. Phil only returned my call after I have fallen asleep.

7. We are happy to have you in our home, but tomorrow, while we are preparing dinner, we hope you did the laundry.

8. I refuse to leave the casino so soon after arriving; it was only twenty minutes.

9. Matilda plans to arrive at four o'clock, when the dancers performed their ballet routine.

10. If you were so concerned about Lauren's decision to get a tattoo of a jack-o-lantern on her neck, then maybe you should have said something before she did so.

EXERCISE TWO

These are examples of questions that you will see on the SAT concerning Verb Tense. Follow the directions below.

IMPROVING SENTENCES
Choose the answer that best improves the sentence.

1. Jane Goodall, a noteworthy environmentalist, <u>beginning her research on the Kasakela Chimpanzee in 1960, in the Gombe Stream National Park</u>.

(A) beginning her research on the Kasakela Chimpanzee in 1960, in the Gombe Stream National Park
(B) who began her research on the Kasakela Chimpanzee in 1960, in the Gombe Stream National Park
(C) began her research on the Kasakela Chimpanzee in 1960, the Gombe Stream National Park
(D) began her research on the Kasakela Chimpanzee in 1960, in the Gombe Stream National Park
(E) beginning her research on the Kasakela Chimpanzee in 1960, living in the Gombe Stream National Park

2. Despite the fact that Thomas Alva Edison received the credit for channeling electricity toward the light bulb, <u>Nikola Tesla arguably contributing as much to developments in electrical engineering as did Edison</u>.

(A) Nikola Tesla arguably contributing as much to developments in electrical engineering as did Edison
(B) but Nikola Tesla arguably contributed as much to developments in electrical engineering as did Edison
(C) Nikola Tesla arguably contributed as much to developments in electrical engineering over Edison
(D) Nikola Tesla arguably contributed as much to developments in electrical engineering as did Edison
(E) Nikola Tesla, who arguably contributed as much to developments in electrical engineering as Edison

IDENTIFYING SENTENCE ERRORS
Choose the answer that correctly identifies the error.

3. Before Wanda realized the <u>error of her</u> ways, she
                   A
<u>was</u> already damaged her reputation as <u>a wise leader</u>
 B   C
and skilled strategist, thus lowering her chances of

<u>winning</u> the election. <u>No error</u>
 D   E

4. Calvin and Queenie enjoy their jobs <u>as archaeologists</u>
                                 A
because digging up the remains of Egyptian tombs

<u>provides</u> both insight into the lives of pharaohs who
 B
<u>were</u> dead for centuries and a close look at an age
 C
<u>long since</u> past. <u>No error</u>
 D   E

ANSWER KEY | **VERB TENSE**
LESSON 8

EXERCISE 1:

1. In 1979, the Islamic Republic of Iran *was* established.

2. Sandy regretted his decision to ignore his parents' curfew: when he *got* home late, they were waiting at the door with a list of punishments.

3. After Olga had thrown me out of her apartment, I thought that perhaps I should not have tried to bathe my pet goat in her shower. *(no error)*

4. Fiona *has been* writing her novel for nine hours straight, and she is still going strong.

5. In 1969, the famous Woodstock concert *attracted* hordes of people.

6. Phil only returned my call after I *had* fallen asleep.

7. We are happy to have you in our home, but tomorrow, while we are preparing dinner, we hope you *will do* the laundry.

8. I refuse to leave the casino so soon after arriving; it *has only been* twenty minutes.

9. Matilda plans to arrive at four o'clock, when the dancers *will perform* their ballet routine.

10. If you were so concerned about Lauren's decision to get a tattoo of a jack-o-lantern on her neck, then maybe you should have said something before she did so. *(no error)*

EXERCISE 2:

1. D

2. D

3. B

4. C

Chapter 10

IDIOM

Idiom

IDIOM LESSON 9

An **Idiom** is simply the customary way of saying a particular phrase. The idioms on the SAT should not to be confused with colloquial expressions such as "all ears" or "across the board." **Instead, an idiomatic error occurs when the preposition is used incorrectly.**

WHEN YOU SEE a preposition or a prepositional phrase underlined, STOP and CHECK:

Is this the correct preposition?

FORMULA: preposition + phrase OR preposition alone

EXAMPLES: *listen to, at the mall, from, of*

LESSON 9.1   IDIOMATIC ERRORS

The best way to master IDIOMATIC ERRORS on the SAT is to keep a list of the idioms, prepositions, and prepositional phrases that you come across in any SAT practice test that you might do.

EXAMPLE

She was arguing *against* her mother. ✘

She was arguing **with** her mother. ✓

When you come across an idiom that is not on your list, use the written idiom in three short and simple sentences in your head and see which preposition you use most often. If it is a different preposition than the one written, you may be looking at an idiom error. But remember to follow the format of the sentence. See below.

LESSON 9.2   INCORRECT PREPOSITION

EXAMPLE   For my birthday, my parents insisted *about* taking me to dinner. ✘

EXPLANATION   To check if the preposition *about* is used correctly, quickly create three sentences in your head using the word (or phrase) before the preposition. Here, that word is *insisted*.

SENTENCE 1: They insisted *on* driving their own car.

SENTENCE 2: She insisted *on* paying me back.

SENTENCE 3: He insisted *on* opening the door for me.

For my birthday, my parents insisted **on** taking me to dinner. ✓

LESSON 9.3   **COLLOQUIAL SPEECH ERRORS**

The SAT will occasionally use COLLOQUIAL SPEECH, or slang, to hide an error.

EXAMPLE   She should of gone to the market herself if she was that hungry. ✗

EXPLANATION   Did you catch the error? The SAT selectively hides the error based on colloquial speech. In this case, *should of* sounds similar to *should've* which is the contraction for the phrase *should have*.

She should of gone to the market herself if she was that hungry. ✗

She should've gone to the market herself is she was that hungry. ✓

She should *have* gone to the market herself if she was that hungry. ✓

Following the principle explained above, **WHEN YOU SEE** *should of, could of,* or *would of,* **these phrases are wrong.**

Use this space for additional notes. The following pages have exercises regarding Idiom.

EXERCISE ONE

DIRECTIONS: Using the strategies you learned on pages 74 - 75, complete the idiomatic phrase.

EXAMPLE:

Johnathan was familiar _*with*_ social media and digital marketing strategies.

1. The defendant was accompanied _____ two police officers.

2. I refuse to be held responsible _____ something I didn't do.

3. She has a tendency _____ cower when someone yells at her.

4. After watching the movie, he was convinced _____ the existence of aliens.

5. The scientist's findings were inconsistent _____ other researchers' results.

6. The actor was celebrated _____ his philanthropic work in developing countries.

7. Eric was criticized _____ being indecisive in making life choices.

8. I prefer iced tea _____ sweetened soda.

9. The record player I bought Bruce looks similar _____ older record players.

10. The students constantly complained _____ the amount of homework they received.

These are examples of questions that you will see on the SAT concerning Idiom. Follow the directions below.

IMPROVING SENTENCES
Choose the answer that best improves the sentence.

1. Some people <u>have a habit with criticizing</u> every small deficiency, but Lynne is able to look past such foibles and focus on only the most pressing problems.

   (A) have a habit with criticizing
   (B) have a habit, and they are criticizing
   (C) have a habit of criticizing
   (D) who have a habit from criticizing
   (E) who have a habit by criticizing

2. <u>If traveling at the Russian countryside</u>, you will discover a series of grand and idiosyncratic military monuments, many of them constructed in the decades after World War II.

   (A) If traveling at the Russian countryside
   (B) When they travel at the Russian countryside
   (C) When one travels through the Russian countryside
   (D) Because you travel despite the Russian countryside
   (E) If you travel through the Russian countryside

IDENTIFYING SENTENCE ERRORS
Choose the answer that correctly identifies the error.

3. Recently, soft drink companies <u>have been reducing</u> the
                                            A
   amount of plastic <u>used to</u> manufacturing bottles,
                        B
   <u>both in order</u> to save money and <u>to protect</u> the
        C   D
   environment. <u>No error</u>
                    E

4. After <u>disappearing by</u> the news for almost two decades,
              A
   <u>the candidate decided</u> to return to the public spotlight
              B
   <u>with a bold</u> and unconventional campaign <u>for a seat</u>
        C   D
   in the Senate. <u>No error</u>
                      E

(ANSWERS ON NEXT PAGE)

Answer Key

EXERCISE 1:

1. The defendant was accompanied ___*by*___ two police officers.

2. I refuse to be held responsible ___*for*___ something I didn't do.

3. She has a tendency ___*to*___ cower when someone yells at her.

4. After watching the movie, he was convinced ___*of*___ the existence of aliens.

5. The scientist's findings were inconsistent ___*with*___ other researchers' results.

6. The actor was celebrated ___*for*___ his philanthropic work in developing countries.

7. Eric was criticized ___*for*___ being indecisive in making life choices.

8. I prefer iced tea ___*to*___ sweetened soda.

9. The record player I bought Bruce looks similar ___*to*___ older record players.

10. The students constantly complained ___*about*___ the amount of homework they received.

EXERCISE 2:

1. C

2. E

3. B

4. A

Chapter 11
DICTION

DICTION LESSON 10

Diction simply means "word choice."

WHEN YOU SEE a word that sounds similar to another word, STOP and CHECK:

"Is this the correct word?"

The SAT may use a word that appears to be the intended word, but does not make sense in context. Sometimes, a word will sound almost right, but not quite. It is usually a word that is commonly confused with another due to spelling or sound.

The best way to combat diction errors is to **KNOW YOUR VOCABULARY.** Generally, only 1 to 2 Diction errors appear on any given test. On the next page is a chart of the most common diction errors on the SAT.

| **LESSON 10.1** | **DICTION** |

A common **DICTION** error is mixing *proceed(s)* and *precede(s)*.
Proceed(s) can function as a verb or noun depending on the context of the sentence:
Proceed(s) as a **VERB** means "to advance." / *Proceeds* as a **NOUN** refers to money.
Precede(s) as a **VERB** will ALWAYS mean "to come before."
Below are examples of diction errors involving the words *proceed(s)* and *precede(s)*.

| **EXAMPLE** | We decided to precede with the business venture even though the market is volatile. ✘ |

| **EXPLANATION** | *Precede* means to come before. We didn't decide *to come before* the business venture. We decided to *advance*, or *continue* with the business venture, or *proceed* with it. |

We decided to **proceed** with the business venture even though the market is volatile. ✓

| **EXAMPLE** | The precedes from the fundraiser helped to build wells in a dozen impoverished villages. ✘ |

| **EXPLANATION** | Here, based on the context of the sentence, we know that we are looking for a word that means *the funds received for charitable purposes*. Therefore, *precedes* is incorrect. The correct word would be *proceeds*. |

The **proceeds** from the fundraiser helped to build wells in a dozen impoverished villages. ✓

COMMON DICTION ERRORS ON THE SAT

ACCEPT To agree or consent to	**EXCEPT** To exclude; to leave out
ADOPT To take in	**ADAPT** To adjust
AFFECT To influence	**EFFECT** (n) result; (v) to bring about
ALLUDE To refer to	**ELUDE** To escape from
ALLUSION An indirect reference (often to literature)	**ILLUSION** An unreal image; a false impression
AMBIVALENT Uncertain, having mixed feelings	**AMBIGUOUS** Unclear
ANECDOTE A short account based on real life experience	**ANTIDOTE** A remedy
ASSURE To comfort in order to dispel doubts	**ENSURE** To confirm; to make certain
COLLABORATE To work together	**CORROBORATE** To confirm
COMPLEMENT An addition that enhances or improves	**COMPLIMENT** Praise
COUNSEL To advise, to offer guidance	**COUNCIL** An advisory body that meets regularly
DEFER To put off; to comply	**REFER** To bring up; to consult
DELUDE Deceive	**DILUTE** To reduce strength
DISCRETE Separate, distinct	**DISCREET** Reserved in speech and action, circumspect
DISINTERESTED Neutral, impartial	**UNINTERESTED** Not interested
ELEGANT Well-designed	**ELOQUENT** To be able to articulate well
ELICIT To draw out or bring forth	**ILLICIT** Not legally allowed
FLAUNT To show off	**FLOUT** To exhibit scorn or contempt
IMMINENT Likely to occur at any moment	**EMINENT** High in rank or repute
INAPT Unsuitable	**INEPT** Unskilled
INEQUITY Inequality	**INIQUITY** Immorality
INHABIT To occupy	**INHIBIT** To constrain
PERSPECTIVE Viewpoint	**PROSPECTIVE** Potential, possible
RELUCTANT Unwilling	**RETICENT** Silent, reserved

EXERCISE ONE

DIRECTIONS: Identify the diction error using the information from pages 80 - 81.

EXAMPLE:

complemented

Using the same color for the furniture ~~complimented~~ the interior decorator's overall aesthetic.

1. The president was finally impeached for flaunting governmental procedures.

2. We decided that it was time to precede to the lodge before it got any darker in the woods.

3. When he eluded to "Big Brother" in his novel, we all knew that he was really talking about communism.

4. We were thrilled to get such an imminent professor on our teaching staff.

5. As an expert, John was used to people referring to his decisions.

6. If the hospital refuses to stock anecdotes for rare spider bites, more people will inevitably die.

7. A euphemism involves deluding harsh criticism in order to sound nicer.

8. The hieroglyphics are essentially ambivalent; scientists must rely on the "Rosetta Stone" to decipher them.

9. We were amazed at the eloquence of her dress since she usually wears jeans and hiking boots.

10. The corroboration was so successful because every department head played a role in the creative process.

EXERCISE
TWO

These are examples of questions that you will see on the SAT concerning Diction. Follow the directions below.

IDENTIFYING SENTENCE ERRORS
Choose the answer that correctly identifies the error.

1. <u>Irritated by</u> his research team's constant missteps,
   A

Professor Hartwick <u>brought the project</u> to a halt
           B

<u>and told</u> his subordinates to develop a <u>more affective</u>
C   D

experimental method. <u>No error</u>
           E

2. We all made a point <u>of complementing</u> Rufus on
           A

<u>his new hairstyle</u>, even though we <u>privately agreed</u>
     B   C

that he <u>did not look</u> particularly attractive with such
        D

short hair. <u>No error</u>
       E

3. Despite <u>her efforts</u>, Beth was unable to <u>illicit</u> a positive
       A   B

response from her young cousin, <u>who refused</u> to talk even
                         C

when offered cookies, candies, and toys <u>as incentives</u>.
                                 D

<u>No error</u>
E

4. In <u>his recent</u> sculptures, controversial artist
    A

<u>Jeff Koons alludes</u> to works <u>of Greek and Roman</u> statuary
      B   C

<u>that are</u> revered by even his harshest critics. <u>No error</u>
 D   E

ANSWER KEY DICTION LESSON 10

EXERCISE 1:

1. The president was finally impeached for ~~flaunting~~ *flouting* the governmental procedures.

2. We decided that it was time to ~~precede~~ *proceed* to the lodge before it got any darker in the woods.

3. When he ~~eluded~~ *alluded* to Big Brother in his novel, we all knew that he was really talking about communism.

4. We were thrilled to get such an ~~imminent~~ *eminent* professor on our teaching staff.

5. As an expert, John was used to people ~~referring~~ *deferring* to his decisions.

6. If the hospital refuses to stock ~~anecdotes~~ *antidotes* for rare spider bites, more people will inevitably die.

7. A euphemism involves ~~deludes~~ *diluting* harsh criticism in order to sound nicer.

8. The hieroglyphics are essentially ~~ambivalent~~ *ambiguous;* scientists must rely on the "Rosetta Stone" to decipher them.

9. We were amazed at the ~~eloquence~~ *elegance* of her dress since she usually wears jeans and hiking boots.

10. The ~~corroboration~~ *collaboration* was so successful because every department head played a role in the creative process.

EXERCISE 2:

1. D

2. A

3. B

4. E

Chapter 12
SENTENCE STRUCTURE

SENTENCE STRUCTURE LESSON 11

SENTENCE STRUCTURE refers to the arrangement of ideas in a sentence. The arrangement should be logical and should adhere to the laws of grammar. If a sentence is illogical, it is necessary to consider the following common problems below. Each problem will have a specific visual clue that will act as a guide to identifying the errors in the sentence.

| LESSON 11.1 | **COMMA SPLICES AND RUN-ON SENTENCES** |

 A COMMA SPLICE occurs when two full sentences (commonly called independent clauses) are combined using only a comma. To fix a comma splice problem on the SAT, you have to use a colon (:), a semi-colon (;), or a transition word (but, and, yet, or, so, for, nor).

EXAMPLE

John went to Vermont to ski, he had a really good time. ✗

John went to Vermont to ski, **and** he had a really good time. ✓

I have taken several yoga classes over the years, my favorite is Vinyasa Yoga. ✗

I have taken several yoga classes over the years, **but** my favorite is Vinyasa Yoga. ✓

 BE CAREFUL when fixing comma splices. Inserting a transition word after the comma fixes the problem, but never insert a transition word *followed by* a comma. This often creates a clause that can stand alone as a sentence. This does not fix the comma splice. See below.

EXAMPLE

Cars are notoriously bad for the environment, *but,* the research and development of alternative fuel have mitigated the automobile's impact on emissions. ✗

Cars are notoriously bad for the environment, **but** the research and development of alternative fuel have mitigated the automobile's impact of emissions. ✓

LESSON 11.2   THE COLON AND SEMI-COLON

Use a SEMI-COLON (;) when joining two closely related independent clauses in a single sentence. When using a semi-colon, make sure that the two adjoining clauses can stand alone as sentences. Avoid using a semi-colon WITH a conjunction.

EXAMPLE

The film's plot was confusing; and the audience members didn't understand it. ✗

The film's plot was confusing; the audience members didn't understand it. ✓

A COLON (:) is used in basically the same way a semi-colon is used, except that a colon implies that an explanation will follow.

EXAMPLE

The house needs a serious renovation and the basement is not structurally sound. **(Clarify more)**

EXPLANATION

The sentence is grammatically correct. However, if you replace *and* with a colon, this replacement clarifies *why* the house needs a serious renovation.

The house needs a serious renovation: the basement is not structurally sound. **(Clear)** ✓

LESSON 11.3   TRANSITION WORDS

A TRANSITION WORD error occurs when the transition word given does not follow the logic of the sentence.

EXAMPLE

She seemed very upset at work today, and she looked happier when she left. ✗

EXPLANATION

The content of the sentence signals a CONTRAST in tone (upset to happier), but the transition word *and* implies agreement. Therefore, we must replace *and* with a word that will follow the logic of the sentence *(but, yet)*.

She seemed very upset at work, ***but*** she looked happier when she left. ✓

Sometimes there will be two similar conjunctions given in the same sentence. Be aware of these errors as they are often disguised. See below.

EXAMPLE

Although it rained at the family picnic, but everyone still had a good time. ✗

EXPLANATION

Although and *but* signify the same relationship shift (rained to good time), so including both transition words causes a redundancy error. Omit one.

Although it rained at the family picnic, everyone still had a good time. ✓
It rained at the family picnic, but everyone still had a good time. ✓

WHEN YOU SEE one of the following in the grammar section, check to make sure that this word is preceded by a semi-colon (;) **if it begins an independent clause.**

However • Therefore • Moreover Consequently • Nevertheless

EXAMPLE	Many people know that eating breakfast is essential, nevertheless, most people skip this meal. ✗
EXPLANATION	In this sentence, *nevertheless* begins the independent clause *most people skip this meal.* Use a semi-colon before *nevertheless* to connect the independent clauses.
	Many people know that eating breakfast is essential; nevertheless, most people skip this meal. ✓

LESSON 11.4   **STANDARD PHRASES**

WHEN YOU SEE the first or second half of a standard phrase underlined, check that the other half is placed appropriately.

The SAT will test you on the correct completion of standard phrases. There are many standard phrases in the English language, but here are some common examples found on the SAT.

STANDARD PHRASE EXAMPLES

NEITHER...NOR	I was neither happy about the service or satisfied by the food at that restaurant. ✗	I was neither happy about the service *nor* satisfied by the food at that restaurant. ✓
EITHER...OR	Either we take the car into the city and hope we find parking and on the other hand we take the train in. ✗	Either we take the car into the city and hope we find parking *or* we take the train in. ✓
NOT ONLY...BUT ALSO	The dogs at the shelter were not only cramped in their cages but in addition to that they were not fed at regular intervals. ✗	The dogs at the shelter were not only cramped in their cages *but also* not fed at regular intervals. ✓
AS...AS	Janet is just as deserving of the teacher of the year award than Jeff. ✗	Janet is just as deserving of the teacher of the year award *as* Jeff. ✓
BOTH...AND	Carol is both jealous of her brother's soccer skill in addition to being mad at him for stealing her ball. ✗	Carol is both jealous of her brother's soccer skill *and* mad at him for stealing her ball. ✓

| LESSON 11.5 | REDUNDANCY |

 REDUNDANCY occurs when words or phrases with the same meaning are repeated.

| EXAMPLE | In the year 1912, ✗ |

| EXPLANATION | *Year* is not needed when a specific year is given. |

In 1912, ✓

| EXAMPLE | Every year the college's alumni gather for the annual jamboree. ✗ |

| EXPLANATION | *Every year* and *annual* mean the same thing. |

Every year the college's alumni gather for the jamboree. ✓
The college's alumni gather for the annual jamboree. ✓

 REASON/BECAUSE/SINCE/WHY
The words REASON, BECAUSE, SINCE, and WHY cannot be in the same sentence. These words all indicate explanation; therefore, it would be redundant to use them in conjunction with one another. If you see these words used in the same sentence, try replacing one of the words with *THAT*.

| EXAMPLE | The *reason* I arrived late was *because* I didn't hear my alarm clock. ✗ |

| EXPLANATION | The *explanation* for my lateness *was that I didn't hear my alarm clock.* Use the word *that* in place of *because*. |

The reason I arrived late was **that** I didn't hear my alarm clock. ✓

Use this space for additional notes. The following pages have exercises regarding Sentence Structure.

12

EXERCISE ONE

DIRECTIONS: Using what you learned on pages 86 - 89, identify the Sentence Structure error: comma splice, semi-colon, colon, redundancy, standard phrase, transition word, or none.
EXAMPLE:
Many argue that the criticism of art is primarily subjective, this often leads to varying opinions on the definition of art. (Comma splice)

1. Even though one studied much more than the other studied, both students similarly got the same grade on the test.

2. Math is Marc's favorite subject, he is naturally very skilled in it.

3. Although it has taken me three decades, I have realized that not everything in life is either black nor white.

4. I don't think teaching, for most, is simply a job; teachers often genuinely care about their students.

5. Because I deactivated my social networking account, but I now feel disconnected from all my friends who live far away.

6. I know it was an irresponsible decision to stay out past curfew, furthermore I had so much fun with my friends that I think it was all worth getting grounded.

7. My favorite book is a thousand pages long: but it still feels too short every time I read it.

8. Joan not only is fully qualified for this job, as well as very highly recommended by her peers.

9. I drink coffee in the morning every single day; but today I decided to eat fruit instead.

10. The reason we scaled the side of the mountain was because we wanted to get to the peak faster.

These are examples of questions that you will see on the SAT concerning Sentence Structure. Follow the directions below.

IMPROVING SENTENCES
Choose the answer that best improves the sentence.

1. The database yielded thousands of links <u>to published articles, only a few of these documents were</u> relevant to the research topic Jerome had chosen.

   (A) to published articles, only a few of these documents were
   (B) to articles that were published, so only a few of these documents were
   (C) to published articles, but only a few of these documents were
   (D) of articles published, they were documents and only a few were also
   (E) and articles published, and only a few of these documents had been

2. The geometry teacher regularly assigns problems that cannot possibly be solved with the assistance <u>of a computer; this institutes</u> a policy prohibiting the use of calculators on exams.

   (A) of a computer; this institutes
   (B) of a computer, he instituted also
   (C) of a computer, instituting
   (D) from computers; and he will institute
   (E) of a computer; moreover, he has instituted

IDENTIFYING SENTENCE ERRORS
Choose the answer that correctly identifies the error.

3. <u>Despite unwise</u> price increases and needless alterations
        A
   <u>to the menu</u>, the <u>deli managed</u> to alienate longtime
       B   C
   customers who had once <u>enjoyed its</u> hearty yet
                       D
   affordable cuisine. <u>No error</u>
                E

4. F. Scott Fitzgerald <u>is most renowned</u> today as
                   A
   the author of *The Great Gatsby*, <u>he was</u> most respected
                            B
   <u>during his own</u> lifetime <u>for the novel</u> *This Side of*
      C   D
   Paradise. <u>No error</u>
          E

ANSWER KEY

SENTENCE STRUCTURE
LESSON 11

EXERCISE 1:

1. redundancy

2. comma splice

3. standard phrase

4. no error

5. transition word

6. transition word

7. colon

8. standard phrase

9. semi-colon

10. redundancy

EXERCISE 2:

1. C

2. E

3. A

4. B

Chapter 13

SUBJUNCTIVE MOOD/HYPOTHETICAL

SUBJUNCTIVE MOOD/HYPOTHETICAL LESSON 12

WHEN YOU SEE "IF" or suggestions/ proposals indicated by the word "THAT" this will indicate the SUBJUNCTIVE MOOD or simply, the HYPOTHETICAL.

he proposes that / he insists that
he asks that / he suggests that

The word *if* or *that* indicates a situation that either **HAS NOT HAPPENED YET** or **DID NOT HAPPEN AT ALL**.

LESSON 12.1	**WISH/CONDITIONAL**
	FORMAT: If I were... I would... OR If I were to.... I would

EXAMPLE	If I **was** stronger, I would be able to lift that heavy box. ✗
EXPLANATION	Based on the context of the sentence, a wish or desire is indicated. Therefore, *was* must be changed to *were*.
	If I ***were*** stronger, I would be able to lift that heavy box. ✓

EXAMPLE	If she **was to** own a farm, she would be self-sustaining. ✗
EXPLANATION	Based on the context of the sentence, she will be self-sustaining on the condition that she owns a farm. Therefore, *was to* must be changed to *were to*.
	If she ***were to*** own a farm, she would be self-sustaining. ✓

LESSON 12.2	**PAST SUBJUNCTIVE**
	FORMAT: If I had.... I would have

EXAMPLE	If he **would have** remembered earlier, he would not have missed his appointment. ✗
EXPLANATION	Notice that this sentence is in PAST TENSE, implying that this DID NOT HAPPEN AT ALL. Therefore, *would have* must be changed to *had*.
	If he ***had*** remembered earlier, he would not have missed his appointment. ✓

LESSON 12.3   **SUGGESTIONS/PROPOSALS**

If you see the word *that*, **stop and check for the following common problems:**

| **EXAMPLE** | The child desperately begs that his mother gives him candy. ✗ |

| **EXPLANATION** | Notice that his mother *has not yet* given him candy.
TO SOLVE, there are TWO steps: |

(1) Find the verb that is being suggested or proposed.

The child desperately begs that his mother *gives* him candy. ✗

He's begging for her *to give*.

(2) Insert the infinitive of the verb (to + verb) WITHOUT the preposition *to*.

The child desperately begs that his mother (t̶o̶ give) him candy.

The child desperately begs that his mother *give* him candy. ✓

Remember that *is* and *are* is conjugated from the infinitive verb *to be*. See below.

| **EXAMPLE** | He proposed that his birthday is celebrated at the community pool. ✗ |

| **EXPLANATION** | **Follow the TWO steps as indicated above:** |

(1) Find the verb that is being suggested or proposed.

He proposed that his birthday *is* celebrated at the community pool.

He is proposing for his birthday *to be*.

(2) Insert the infinitive of the verb (to + verb) WITHOUT the preposition to.

He proposed that his birthday (t̶o̶ be) celebrated at the community pool.

He proposed that his birthday *be* celebrated at the community pool. ✓

Would indicates a situation that is still possible. *Would have* indicates a situation that is a missed opportunity. *Will* indicates a definite future.

EXAMPLE	If you were to keep these tips in mind, you *would* be well-prepared.
	If you had kept these tips in mind, you *would have* been better prepared.
	If you keep these tips in mind, you *will* be well-prepared.

EXERCISE ONE

DIRECTIONS: Correct the sentences using the strategies from pages 94 - 95 if needed.

EXAMPLE:

were
If it ~~was~~ more docile, Dorothy's horse would be perfect for equestrian training.

1. If Jackson had wrapped his elbow before he played, he would not have suffered from severe muscle strain.

2. If he was alive, he would be proud of his son.

3. I wish I was still living in my hometown, Cincinnati.

4. The manager insists that the parking lot is locked at night.

5. The board of directors recommends that he joins the special committee.

6. I wish the vacation was longer.

7. If I would have known Petunia's real intentions, I would have insisted on a prenuptial agreement.

8. If I was an Academy Award winner, I would be more confident in producing my own work.

9. If he were to invite the neighbors to his mother's home for Easter, his sister would be upset.

10. If I was Lee, I would play the guitar every day.

11. I suggest that the last applicant plays the piano for the audition.

12. I propose that John is asked to sing.

These are examples of questions that you will see on the SAT concerning Subjunctive Mood/Hypothetical. Follow the directions below.

IMPROVING SENTENCES
Choose the answer that best improves the sentence.

1. The committee suggested that the motion <u>is passed today if we want to meet our imminent deadlines</u>.

  (A) is passed today if we want to meet our imminent deadlines

  (B) being passed today if we want to imminently meet our deadlines

  (C) be passed today if we want to meet our imminent deadlines

  (D) was passed today if we want to meet our deadlines that are imminent

  (E) will be passed today if want to meet our imminent deadlines

2. I propose <u>that the security staff guards the party's entrance</u> while the movie stars gather for the event.

  (A) that the security staff guards the party's entrance

  (B) that the security staff guard the party's entrance

  (C) when the security staff guarded the entrance of the party

  (D) that the security staff guarding the entrance of the party

  (E) that the security staff guarded the party's entrance

IDENTIFYING SENTENCE ERRORS
Choose the answer that correctly identifies the error.

3. Luckily, the final nursing exam, which <u>had been</u>
                                        A

  <u>scheduled</u> for this October, <u>would be</u> postponed <u>for</u> a
  B   C   D

  few weeks due to new student registrations. <u>No error</u>
                                                E

4. <u>It is</u> clear that most of the constituents in the inner cities
  A

  <u>will have voted</u> for Julia Sanchez <u>if</u> she had taken a more
      B   C

  liberal <u>approach to</u> charter schools. <u>No error</u>
        D   E

(ANSWERS ON NEXT PAGE)

ANSWER KEY **SUBJUNCTIVE MOOD/HYPOTHETICAL**
LESSON 12

EXERCISE 1:

1. If Jackson had wrapped his elbow before he played, he would not have suffered from severe muscle strain. *(no error)*

2. If he *were* alive, he would be proud of his son.

3. I wish I *were* still living in my hometown, Cincinnati.

4. The manager insists that the parking lot *be* locked at night.

5. The board of directors recommends that he *join* the special committee.

6. I wish the vacation *were* longer.

7. If I *had* known Petunia's real intentions, I would have insisted on a prenuptial agreement.

8. If I *were* an Academy Award winner, I would be more confident in producing my own work.

9. If he were to invite the neighbors to his mother's home for Easter, his sister would be upset. *(no error)*

10. If I *were* Lee, I would play the guitar every day.

11. I suggest that the last applicant *play* the piano for the audition.

12. I propose that John *be* asked to sing.

EXERCISE 2:

1. C

2. B

3. C

4. B

Chapter 14

GRAMMAR TECHNIQUE

GRAMMAR TECHNIQUE

Before we explain the Grammar Technique steps, let's review the basic format of the SAT. Each SAT has two Grammar sections. (Occasionally, you'll see an additional 25 minute experimental section.)

SECTION 1 Time–25 minutes 35 Questions	SECTION 2 Time–10 minutes 14 Questions
QUESTION TYPES Improving Sentences Identifying Sentence Errors Improving Paragraphs	**QUESTION TYPES** Improving Sentences

IN ORDER TO USE THE TECHNIQUE, YOU WILL NEED TO APPLY TWO STEPS:

(1.) VPA RULE

CHECK FOR ALL **V**ERBS, **P**RONOUNS, AND **A**DJECTIVES/**A**DVERBS.

EXPLANATION:

A. VPA mistakes are the most prevalent types

B. Verb, Pronoun, Adjective/Adverb mistakes are easily hidden because of wrong colloquial speech and slang patterns, interrupters, and prepositional phrases that cause the ear to hear agreement when it is non-existent.

The test taker must STOP on all VPA applicable words and check the usage. In other words, before choosing "A" or "E," check the verb against the subject, the pronoun against the subject or another pronoun, adjective against the noun, and adverb against the verb or adjective.

YOU WILL NOT HEAR THESE MISTAKES WITHOUT ACTUALLY CHECKING!

(2.) WRITING EDITS

ALWAYS WRITE AN ACTUAL EDIT ON THE SENTENCE OR WORD IN QUESTION.

EXPLANATION:

A. For Improving Sentences, these edits will quicken your process of elimination. If you change "is" to "are," you can quickly eliminate (without reading) all of the choices with "is."

B. For Identifying Sentence Errors, your written edits will enable you to apply a "fail safe." The "fail safe" allows you to check your edit within the context of the entire sentence. You will do this by reading the sentence with your edit. What sounded correct in your head may not look correct when you see the edit in the sentence.

* All of these written edits should follow the rules of our 12 lessons. This will prevent you from choosing an answer with a "style" change, and ensure that your choice is grammatically correct and in line with the original meaning of the sentence.

GRAMMAR TECHNIQUE STEPS

IMPROVING SENTENCES

A portion of the sentence (or the entire sentence) is underlined. Below the sentence are several choices. Choice A, or *as is*, indicates no error in the sentence.

1. Read the entire sentence.

2. If you see an error, make an edit on the actual sentence with your pencil.

3. Read the edit with the sentence.

4. If the edit works, eliminate choices that do not have this edit or a variation of this edit.

5. If more than one choice works with your edit, always pick the answer that is most succinct and adheres to the original meaning of the sentence.

6. If considering Choice A, APPLY THE VPA RULE.

7. If VPA does not reveal any hidden errors, select Choice A.

Choice **"A"** will always be the same as the underlined portion.

1. What I have experienced while living in Manhattan is drastically different ~~from living~~ in New Jersey.

(A) from living in New Jersey
(B) from my experience of New Jersey
(C) than experiencing living in New Jersey
(D) than the experience of living in New Jersey
(E) from what I have experienced while living in New Jersey

Make edits on the actual sentence:

from what I have experienced while

IDENTIFYING SENTENCE ERRORS

The underlined portions of the sentence are the choices. You must identify the error. Choice E indicates no error in the sentence.

1. Read the entire sentence.

2. If you see an error, make an edit on the actual word or phrase with your pencil.

3. If the edit is NEEDED to improve the sentence, then select that choice as the error.

4. If considering Choice E, APPLY THE VPA RULE.

5. If VPA does not reveal any hidden errors, select Choice E.

Choice **"E"** will always be "No Error."

1. Art and music <u>are</u> some <u>of</u> life's greatest pleasures
         A   B
but <u>I</u> feel that music is the m~~o~~st accessible.
C   D *more*
<u>No error</u>
E

Make edits on the actual sentence:

Do not be afraid of the "no error" choice (A or E depending on the question type). There can be several "no error" choices in a row. There is not a set amount of "no error" answers per section.

IMPROVING PARAGRAPHS

This rough draft of an essay contains multiple mistakes. The questions that follow examine parts of the essay that you must improve. If the question does not have a "no error" choice (commonly seen as *leave it as it is* or *as it is now*) then you must assume that the sentence must be improved.

✓ Do NOT mistake this for a critical reading passage.

✓ Do NOT read the entire essay before answering the questions.

1. GO to first question and follow the directions.
   - Each question will require a contextual understanding of the sentence in the question.

2. Read the sentence before and after the sentence in the question.
   - Example: If the question examines sentence (3), read sentence (2) and sentence (4).

3. Check for CONTINUITY and COHESION when eliminating choices. Use the grammar rules that you have just learned.

4. If you do not see an error, APPLY THE VPA RULE to reveal any hidden errors in the sentence.

   EXAMPLE: If you see a pronoun, check the subject which may be in the sentence before. Do they agree in number?

   EXAMPLE: If you see a verb, check the sentences before and after. Do the tenses agree?

(1) Herman Melville's massive novel *Moby-Dick* was written and published in the middle of the nineteenth century. (2) Since this time, this book will reach the undisputed status of a classic, even though very few people have read Melville's 500-page story from front to back. (3) Most of the people who have read it are college professors and students in American literature courses. (4) The answer is ironic, yet most people are infinitely fascinated by books that they may never have the time to read.

(5) *Moby-Dick* is only one example of an immensely long and difficult book that intrigues a huge group of readers. (6) People react similarly to novels like Leo Tolstoy's *Anna Karenina* and Thomas Mann's *The Magic Mountain*, both of these books are over seven hundred pages long, a number that can both drive potential readers away and grab their attention. (7) But these aren't even the most extreme cases. (8) Even fewer readers will attempt to read Samuel Richardson's novel *Clarissa* (a stunning 1500 pages) or Marcel Proust's masterpiece *In Search of Lost Time* (a staggering 3200 pages). (9) Nobody would doubt that these are great works of literature, but many has a logical fear that reading this much would be, to rephrase Proust's title, "time lost."

30. In context, what is the best way to deal with sentence 2?

(A) Leave it as it is.
(B) Delete the sentence.
(C) Use "but" at the end of the sentence 2 to link it with sentence 3.
(D) Place it after sentence 3.
(E) Change "will reach" to "has reached".

You will not see "No Error" but will see "Leave it as it is" or "as it is now" instead.

Always read the sentence before and after the referenced sentence.

NOW YOU KNOW THE FOUNDATIONS OF SAT GRAMMAR

✓ Apply that knowledge and the VPA rule during your process of elimination.

✓ Use the IES Grammar Technique on the Practice Tests in this book.

✓ Good luck!

TIPS Avoid the trap of selecting a multiple choice answer because it appears to improve the sentence. Sometimes what appears to be an improvement actually lacks continuity with the sentences before and after. Always make sure that your selected answer choice is based on contextual backup.

GRAMMAR REVIEW
Before proceeding to the practice tests, correct and/or identify the errors in the following sentences.

GRAMMAR LESSON	EXERCISE
1. SUBJECT/VERB AGREEMENT	Neither of the girls are coming to the party.
2. PARALLELISM	I went walking, hiking, and I went swimming. Her happiness was equal to his being clever.
3. COMPARISON	I prefer the reading of classic fiction to non-fiction. They want to be a lifeguard. I have less dollars than you. Between Jack, Mary, and I things are good. Jack is the best of the two of us.
4 (I). SUBJECT/PRONOUN	Everyone wants their way.
4 (II). PRONOUN CASE	John and me went to the store. John, Steve, and Ken went to the park and he fell. I did better than him.
5. DANGLING MODIFIER	Having driven all night, the bed looked so inviting to John.
6. ADJECTIVE/ADVERB	The girl runs quick. The girl is quick.
7. IRREGULAR VERB	He swum all afternoon. She would have wrote the letter if she had had time.
8. VERB TENSE	In 1969, she is happy to have met him.
9. IDIOM	Listening at the music relaxes me. We all agreed to seeing the same movie.
10. DICTION	She was reticent to ride the huge roller coaster. I alluded the cops after robbing the bank.
11. SENTENCE STRUCTURE	I was very happy, I loved life. She was not only a good musician, and a good tennis player. She was neither happy or sad. He was very angry but she was very mad too. I put sugar in my coffee: I like long books. Every two weeks, I receive my bi-weekly paycheck. His shirt is too short in length.
12. SUBJUNCTIVE MOOD/ HYPOTHETICAL	If she was finished cleaning the house, she would have relaxed. I suggest that Austin wears his seatbelt.

(ANSWERS ON NEXT PAGE)

Answer Key

GRAMMAR LESSON	EXERCISE
1. SUBJECT/VERB	Neither of the girls **is** coming to the party.
2. PARALLELISM	I went walking, hiking, and ~~I went~~ swimming. **(omit "I went")** Her happiness was equal to his **cleverness**.
3. COMPARISON	I prefer the reading of classic fiction to **that of** non-fiction. They want to be **lifeguards**. I have **fewer** dollars than you. **Among** Jack, Mary, and **me** things are good. Jack is the **better** of the two of us.
4 (I). SUBJECT/PRONOUN	Everyone wants **his or her** way.
4 (II). PRONOUN CASE	John and **I** went to the store. John, Steve, and Ken went to the park and **he** fell. **(ambiguous)** I did better than **he**.
5. DANGLING MODIFIER	Having driven all night, **John found the bed so inviting.**
6. ADJECTIVE/ADVERB	The girl runs **quickly**. The girl is quick. **(no error)**
7. IRREGULAR VERB	He **swam** all afternoon. She would have **written** the letter if she had had time.
8. VERB TENSE	In 1969, she **was** happy to have met him.
9. IDIOM	Listening **to** the music relaxed me. We all agreed **on** seeing the same movie.
10. DICTION	She was **reluctant** to ride the huge roller coaster. I **eluded** the cops after robbing the bank.
11. SENTENCE STRUCTURE	I was very happy, **and** I loved life. She was not only a good musician, **but also** a good tennis player. She was neither happy **nor** sad. He was very angry **and** she was very mad too. I put sugar in my coffee: ~~I like long books.~~ **(colon requires explanation)** Every two weeks, I receive my **~~bi-weekly~~** paycheck. **(redundancy)** His shirt is too short ~~in length~~. **(redundancy; *short* already implies length)**
12. SUBJUNCTIVE MOOD/ HYPOTHETICAL	If she **had** finished cleaning the house, she would have relaxed. I suggest that Austin **wear** his seatbelt.

How did you do? If you missed any of the review exercises, consider re-reading the lessons before attempting the practice tests. It is vital that you know all 12 grammar lessons in order to effectively increase your accuracy, speed, and efficient use of technique.

PART II
PRACTICE TESTS

Chapter 15
PRACTICE TEST 1

SECTION 1
Time–25 minutes
35 Questions

1. Writing social media entries for an established company <u>requires brevity, liveliness, and it requires also precision</u>.

   (A) requires brevity, liveliness, and it requires also precision
   (B) requires brevity, liveliness, and precision
   (C) require brevity, liveliness, and they require precision
   (D) requires brevity, liveliness, but it also requires precision
   (E) requires liveliness and being precise and brief as well

2. In response to recent cultural trends promoting self-acceptance, weight-loss programs now highlight living healthy <u>rather than to look attractive</u>.

   (A) rather than to look attractive
   (B) rather than what it was, which was looking attractive
   (C) rather than what it is supposed to be, looking attractive
   (D) rather than looking attractive
   (E) rather to be looking attractive

3. The mental disorder known as <u>schizophrenia, usually confused with multiple personality disorder because</u> few individuals possess the expert training required to distinguish the two.

   (A) schizophrenia, usually confused with multiple personality disorder because
   (B) schizophrenia, usually confused with multiple personality disorder and
   (C) schizophrenia, usually confused with multiple personality disorder who
   (D) schizophrenia, usually confused with multiple personality disorder by one because
   (E) schizophrenia is usually confused with multiple personality disorder because

4. <u>The student activists protesting for a long time, they</u> decided to continue their resistance to political institutions that they felt were unjust and oppressive.

   (A) The student activists protesting for a long time, they
   (B) They, protesting for a long time, the student activists
   (C) Having already protested for a long time, the student activists
   (D) To protest for a long time, the student activists
   (E) The student activists protested for a long time, they

5. <u>Larger governments, often by covert methods, can disseminate its</u> cultural ideologies under the guise of democratic revolution.

   (A) Larger governments, often by covert methods, can disseminate its
   (B) Often by covert methods, larger governments can disseminate their
   (C) Covert methods are often used by larger governments who disseminate its
   (D) Larger governments were often covertly methodical from their dissemination of
   (E) Using methods that were often covert, larger governments can be disseminating its

6. The independent film industry's struggles, <u>which continue to multiply due to growing tax credits for major studio pictures, highlights</u> the troubling possibility that Hollywood is being reduced to providing only crass and commerce-oriented entertainment.

   (A) which continue to multiply due to growing tax credits for major studio pictures, highlights
   (B) which continued to be multiplied by major studio pictures due to its growing tax credits, highlights
   (C) multiplied by major studio pictures that grow due to tax credits, highlighting
   (D) multiplied by major studio pictures where growth is due to tax credits, highlight
   (E) which continue to multiply due to growing tax credits for major studio pictures, highlight

7. Finding obscure sources in a public university's large library is usually not as difficult as <u>finding these sources</u> in a private college's small library.

    (A) finding these sources
    (B) that of finding sources
    (C) for finding sources
    (D) for sources to be found
    (E) are finding those sources

8. <u>Known for her criticism of the prison industrial complex, Angela Davis's 2003 book supports her analysis with direct evidence and philosophical insight.</u>

    (A) Known for her criticism of the prison industrial complex, Angela Davis's 2003 book supports her analysis with direct evidence and philosophical insight.
    (B) Angela Davis's 2003 book criticizes the prison industrial complex, which supports her analysis with direct evidence and philosophical insight.
    (C) Known for her direct evidence and philosophical insight, the criticism of Angela Davis is analyzed in her 2003 book on the prison industrial complex.
    (D) Angela Davis, in 2003, detailed her criticism of the prison industrial complex by analyzing into direct evidence and philosophical insight.
    (E) Known for her criticism of the prison industrial complex, Angela Davis supports her analysis with direct evidence and philosophical insight in her 2003 book.

9. Splitting the single dormitory room <u>between Jackson, Patrick, and I is proving to be a seriously difficult task.</u>

    (A) between Jackson, Patrick, and I is proving to be a seriously difficult task
    (B) between Jackson, Patrick, and I has proven to be a seriously difficult task
    (C) among Jackson, Patrick, and me is proving to be a seriously difficult task
    (D) among Jackson, Patrick, and I are proving to be seriously difficult tasks
    (E) for Jackson, Patrick, and myself is proving to be a seriously difficult task

10. <u>Despite the harsh outcry against her iron rule, the country's economic turmoil was resolved and the empress gained favor with her subjects.</u>

    (A) Despite the harsh outcry against her iron rule, the country's economic turmoil was resolved and the empress gained favor with her subjects.
    (B) The empress, despite the harsh outcry against her iron rule, gained favor with her subjects by resolving the country's economic turmoil.
    (C) Despite the harsh outcry against her iron rule, the empress resolves the country's economic turmoil and by this gained favor with her subjects.
    (D) The empress, having resolved the country's economic turmoil, gained favor by her subjects despite the harsh outcry against her iron rule.
    (E) The country's economic turmoil was resolved by the empress's rule which, despite the harsh outcry against that, thereby gaining favor with her subjects.

11. Dolphins, proven to show characteristics that we normally associate with human behavior, <u>is often discussed in arguments against behaviorism, a branch of philosophical study that concludes that psychology is the science of behavior, not the study of the mind.</u>

    (A) is often discussed in arguments against behaviorism, a branch of philosophical study that concludes that psychology is the science of behavior, not the study of the mind
    (B) are often discussed in an argument against behaviorism, it is concluded that psychology is the science of behavior and not the mind
    (C) was often discussed in arguments of behaviorism, which was a branch of philosophical study concluding that psychology is the science of behavior but not the mind
    (D) have been argued in discussions against behaviorism, that is a branch of philosophical study concluding that psychology is the science of behavior and the mind
    (E) are often discussed in arguments surrounding behaviorism, a branch of philosophical study that concludes that psychology is the science of behavior, not the study of the mind

Practice Test 1

12. While <u>flying above</u> the storm was thrilling, <u>it was</u>
              A   B

also frightening, and the passengers were relieved

when the plane <u>final</u> landed <u>on</u> the tarmac. <u>No error</u>
               C   D   E

13. It <u>was fortunate that</u> the interpreter, despite her
          A

limited schedule, <u>was available</u> <u>to decipher</u> the
                   B   C

cryptic message <u>quick</u> and efficiently. <u>No error</u>
              D   E

14. The renowned chef from Switzerland

<u>will have refrained</u> from <u>using tomatoes in his</u>
         A   B

tasting menu <u>if</u> he had known that his star client
           C

was completely allergic to <u>them</u>. <u>No error</u>
                    D   E

15. <u>Seeking to</u> investigate the plausibility
     A

of <u>artificial intelligence</u>, Alan Turing developed a
        B

test <u>to determine</u> whether a machine can produce
      C

answers that approximate <u>those of a human</u>.
                        D

<u>No error</u>
  E

16. According to a recent survey of private business

owners, the best employees are those <u>which</u>
                                 A

<u>consistently try</u> to promote the welfare of the
     B

company, not <u>those with</u> the <u>most professional</u>
               C   D

experience. <u>No error</u>
        E

17. <u>With the utmost courage</u>, the knight valiantly
     A

fought <u>to the king's</u> tyrannical taxation and
        B

championed measures that <u>would dismantle</u> rigid
                    C

class divisions between commoners <u>and nobles</u>.
                            D

<u>No error</u>
  E

18. For many residents <u>of troubled</u> urban areas,
                    A

minimum wage work is a <u>primary source of</u> income
                         B

<u>rather than</u> a means <u>about affording</u> pleasant
  C   D

luxuries or gaining more varied life experience.

<u>No error</u>
  E

19. The deployment <u>of</u> missile <u>strikes in</u> heavily
                A   B

populated areas <u>have caused</u> tremendous
               C

setbacks in negotiations between the two

<u>already antagonistic</u> countries. <u>No error</u>
     D   E

20. Some of the students <u>who claim</u> that
                A

the new professor's lectures are unclear

<u>would most likely</u> see the situation differently
           B

if they <u>would actually complete</u> the assigned
  C   D

readings before class. <u>No error</u>
               E

110

21. Jessica, <u>often mistaken</u> for her twin sister Ramona,
             A

<u>believed</u> that the only way <u>to distinguish</u> herself
     B   C

<u>to</u> her sister was to dye her hair blonde. <u>No error</u>
D   E

22. The staring contest between my older brother

and <u>I</u> started as a way to determine <u>who would</u>
     A   B

<u>receive</u> the last cookie, but after our uncle baked
     C

<u>more of them</u> we decided to give up. <u>No error</u>
       D   E

23. The college entrance examinations were considered

easy by <u>most</u>, but Oliver found that <u>these tests</u> did
           A   B

not <u>serve</u> as <u>indications to</u> his true mathematical
       C   D

aptitude. <u>No error</u>
                 E

24. Undoubtedly, the current curriculum's drawbacks <u>are</u>
                                                              A

<u>their</u> lack of informative material as well as absence
  B

of <u>educational oversight</u> in the composition <u>of</u> the
           C   D

lesson plans. <u>No error</u>
                       E

25. The demolition of the downtown movie theater,

<u>originally</u> <u>planned for</u> next year, <u>would be</u>
     A   B   C

permanently canceled because of the immense

backlash from townsfolk <u>who</u> consider the theater a
                                    D

landmark. <u>No error</u>
                   E

26. Attention <u>to</u> details <u>are</u> not, as many workers
                   A   B

believe, simply <u>another way</u> for the employer
                        C

<u>to indirectly test</u> the employees. <u>No error</u>
        D   E

27. For any child <u>who</u> desires to go to the parade, it <u>is</u>
                       A   B

imperative that <u>they are</u> accompanied by <u>an adult</u>.
                        C   D

<u>No error</u>
    E

28. Dragons and griffins were often regarded

<u>as a symbol</u> of power in <u>ancient cultures</u> because
       A   B

<u>they possessed</u> large stature, expansive wings,
        C

<u>and ferocious talons</u>. <u>No error</u>
         D   E

29. <u>After analyzing the data,</u> I <u>concluded that</u>
                   A   B

prospective engineers are often required <u>to choose</u>
                                                    C

between a career in chemical engineering <u>or one in</u>
                                                    D

biological engineering. <u>No error</u>
                                 E

(1) Did you know that there is an author who is equally loved by children and adults all over the world? **(2)** Perhaps you have heard of him because his name is Roald Dahl and his books have been made into popular movies, including some with wild special effects. **(3)** If you think it's incredible that Dahl's books have such large appeal, take a look at his lifestyle. **(4)** He lived adventures as interesting as anything you will find in his novels *Charlie and the Chocolate Factory* and *James and the Giant Peach*.

    (5) During World War II, Dahl was a fighter pilot, constantly putting his life in danger to protect his home country. **(6)** And when he turned to fiction, Dahl took a different kind of risk. **(7)** His books criticized the world of adults and prized characters such as dreamers, freethinkers, and rebels against everything that makes life uninteresting. **(8)** Some people believe that Dahl's writings speak up for the 1960s counterculture and other movements, just using fantasy instead of real-life politics.

    (9) One great example of Dahl's spirit of adventure is *James and the Giant Peach*. **(10)** In this novel, a young boy named James runs away from his cruel aunts and makes new friends: a group of huge insects with clever and wonderful ideas. **(11)** Oddly enough, Dahl had originally considered calling this book *James and the Giant Cherry*. **(12)** Both adults and children can relate to this desire to live in a way that isn't predictable, and to meet fascinating people who have valuable lessons to teach.

30. What is the best way to deal with the word "because" in sentence 2?

    (A) Replace it with a comma.
    (B) Replace it with "and on the other hand".
    (C) Replace it with a colon.
    (D) Replace it with "furthermore".
    (E) Replace it with "yet".

31. Of the following, which is the best way to combine sentences 3 and 4 (reproduced below)?

If you think it's incredible that Dahl's books have such large appeal, take a look at his lifestyle. He lived adventures as interesting as anything you will find in his novels Charlie and the Chocolate Factory *and* James and the Giant Peach.

    (A) If you think it's incredible that Dahl's books have such large appeal, just taking a look at his novels *Charlie and the Chocolate Factory* and *James and the Giant Peach* will find adventures as interesting as anything he lived.
    (B) If you think it's incredible that Dahl's books have such large appeal, you might want to consider Dahl's lifestyle, which was as interesting as anything you will find in his novels *Charlie and the Chocolate Factory* and *James and the Giant Peach*.
    (C) If you think it's incredible that Dahl's books have such large appeal, his novels *Charlie and the Chocolate Factory* and *James and the Giant Peach* are important for you to look at, with its adventures as interesting as anything Dahl lived.
    (D) If you think it's incredible that Dahl's books have such large appeal, just take a look at his adventures as interesting as anything one will have found his novels *Charlie and the Chocolate Factory* and *James and the Giant Peach*.
    (E) If you think it's incredible that Dahl's books have such large appeal, taking a look at his adventures as interesting as anything you will find in his novels *Charlie and the Chocolate Factory* and *James and the Giant Peach*.

32. In context, which of the following is the best way to revise the underlined portion of sentence 6 (reproduced below)?

And when he turned to fiction, Dahl took a different kind of risk.

(A) When he turned to fiction, however, Dahl took
(B) At last, when he was turning to fiction, Dahl took
(C) He turned to fiction, yet Dahl took
(D) Beyond turning to fiction, Dahl took
(E) In addition, he turned to fiction, and Dahl took

33. Of the following, which is the best version of sentence 8 reproduced below?

Some people believe that Dahl's writings speak up for the 1960s counterculture and other movements, just using fantasy instead of real-life politics.

(A) (As it is now)
(B) Some people believe that Dahl's writings, which focus on fantasy instead of real-life politics, speak for the 1960s counterculture and other movements.
(C) Using fantasy instead of real-life politics, Dahl's writings speak up for the 1960s counterculture and other movements according to some.
(D) Some people believe that Dahl's writings, by using fantasy instead of real-life politics, speaks up for the 1960s counterculture and other movements.
(E) Dahl's writings used fantasy instead of real-life politics, whereby some people believe to speak up for the 1960s counterculture and other movements.

34. Where would it be best to insert the following additional sentence?

As a member of this fellowship, James is empowered to create daring plans of his own; on multiple occasions, he even saves the lives of his bug-like comrades.

(A) After sentence 4
(B) After sentence 8
(C) After sentence 9
(D) After sentence 10
(E) After sentence 12

35. Which of the following sentences can be omitted to most effectively improve the passage as a whole?

(A) Sentence 4
(B) Sentence 5
(C) Sentence 7
(D) Sentence 11
(E) Sentence 12

STOP
**If you finish before time is called, you may check your work on this section only.
Do not turn to any other section in the test.**

15 15 15 15 15 15 15

Unauthorized copying or reuse of any part of this page is illegal.

SECTION 2
Time—10 minutes
14 Questions

1. Often mistaken for a dolphin because of its high pitched twitter, <u>the Beluga whale, it is one of two marine mammals that has adapted to arctic temperatures.</u>

   (A) the Beluga whale, it is one of two marine mammals that has adapted to arctic temperatures
   (B) Beluga whales are one of the two marine mammals that was adapted to arctic temperatures
   (C) it is one of the two marine mammals that has adapted to arctic temperatures, as the Beluga whale
   (D) the Beluga whale is one of the two marine mammals that have adapted to arctic temperatures
   (E) Beluga whales, they are one of the two marine mammals that have adapted to arctic temperatures

2. <u>Because writing requires discipline, commitment, and being talented,</u> procrastinating authors often fail to complete their novels in time to satisfy publishers' deadlines and expectations.

   (A) Because writing requires discipline, commitment, and being talented
   (B) Although writing requires discipline, commitment, and talent
   (C) Since writing requires discipline, commitment, and talent
   (D) Writing requires being disciplined, committed, and talented
   (E) With discipline, commitment, and talent when you write

3. <u>The fashion designer usually crafting dresses for the seasonal showcases in New York City, where</u> the fashion industry is known to thrive.

   (A) The fashion designer usually crafting dresses for the seasonal showcases in New York City, where
   (B) The fashion designer usually crafts dresses for the seasonal showcases in New York City, where
   (C) Usually the fashion designer crafting dresses for the seasonal showcase of New York City, where
   (D) In New York City, the fashion designer usually crafting dresses for the seasonal showcases that
   (E) The fashion designer usually crafts dresses for the seasonal showcases in New York City, although

4. Maintaining the kitchen at room temperature, measuring precisely, and most importantly, <u>the folded egg whites are</u> necessary steps that cannot be skipped while making a soufflé.

   (A) the folded egg whites are
   (B) to fold the egg white is
   (C) the fold of egg whites is
   (D) folding egg whites was through
   (E) folding the egg whites are

5. At the end of Kazuo Ishiguro's science fiction novel *Never Let Me Go*, a clone's organs are harvested by a team of doctors and <u>storing into a repository to mitigate medical illness.</u>

   (A) storing into a repository to mitigate medical illness
   (B) were stored in a repository in order to mitigate medical illness
   (C) are stored in a repository in order to mitigate medical illness
   (D) have been stored in a repository which will mitigate medical illness
   (E) mitigating medical illness through the repository storage

6. <u>Although many philosophers, like John Searle, consider artificial intelligence to be currently impossible, but Oxford scholar Roger Penrose disagrees with this notion.</u>

   (A) Although many philosophers, like John Searle, consider artificial intelligence to be currently impossible, but Oxford scholar Roger Penrose disagrees with this notion.
   (B) Many philosophers, such as John Searle, consider artificial intelligence to be currently impossible because Oxford scholar Roger Penrose disagrees with this notion.
   (C) John Searle and Roger Penrose, an Oxford scholar, consider artificial intelligence to be currently impossible though Penrose also disagrees with this notion.
   (D) Since John Searle considers artificial intelligence to be currently impossible, Roger Penrose, an Oxford scholar like many philosophers, disagrees with this notion.
   (E) Many philosophers, like John Searle, consider artificial intelligence to be currently impossible, but Oxford scholar Roger Penrose disagrees with this notion.

7. Michel Foucault, a prominent French philosopher who examined the relationship between knowledge and power, <u>and was publishing several books on the history of modernity</u>.

(A) and was publishing several books on the history of modernity

(B) that published several books about the history of modernity

(C) but published several books on the history of modernity

(D) published several books on the history of modernity

(E) and several books on the history of modernity having been published

8. <u>The researcher, having examined his subjects with the utmost care, was distressed to discover</u> the symptoms of a raging pandemic disease.

(A) The researcher, having examined his subjects with the utmost care, was distressed to discover

(B) The researcher examines his subjects with the utmost care, he had been distressed to discover

(C) The subjects are examined with the utmost care by the researcher, distressed to discover

(D) The researcher, who examines his subjects with the utmost care, distressed to discover

(E) The subjects, examined by the researcher with the utmost care, have distress to discover

9. In the 1990s, rap music became more popular in suburban <u>areas, whereas advancing finally into the mainstream during the early 2000s</u>.

(A) areas, whereas advancing finally into the mainstream during the early 2000s

(B) areas with rap finally advancing into the mainstream during the early 2000s

(C) areas, finally it had advanced into the mainstream during the early 2000s

(D) areas, finally advanced into the mainstream during the early 2000s

(E) areas, and finally advanced into the mainstream during the early 2000s

10. As president of the cinema club, Diane implemented new policies that would require basic knowledge of film for new <u>members, and they improved the intellectual discussions within the club</u>.

(A) members, and they improved the intellectual discussions within the club

(B) members, they improved the intellectual discussions within the club

(C) members; improving the intellectual discussions within the club

(D) members; these policies improved the intellectual discussions within the club

(E) members and they improved their intellectual discussions because of this within the club

11. <u>Although the plight of the Native Americans may seem confined to the borders of the United States, settler colonialism</u> is prevalent in many countries where the indigenous population has been displaced.

(A) Although the plight of the Native Americans may seem confined to the borders of the United States, settler colonialism

(B) The plight of the Native Americans may seem confined to the borders of the United States, settler colonialism

(C) Even if the plight of the Native Americans may seem confined to the borders of the United States, regardless settler colonialism

(D) Although the plight of the Native Americans may seem confining between the borders of the United Sates, settler colonialism

(E) The plight of the Native Americans is not only confined within the borders of the United States, but also settler colonialism

12. The junior student government is planning <u>not only to book a fancy hotel but also finding great live music</u> for their future senior prom.

(A) not only to book a fancy hotel but also finding great live music

(B) not only finding great live music but also booking a fancy hotel

(C) not only to book a fancy hotel but also found great live music

(D) not only to book a fancy hotel but also to find great live music

(E) not only great live music but also booked a fancy hotel

115

15 15 15 15 15 15 15

Unauthorized copying or
reuse of any part of this
page is illegal.

13. As president of the Women's Christian Temperance Union, <u>Frances Willard believed that the only way to secure voting rights for women was to institutionalize the prohibition of alcohol.</u>

(A) Frances Willard believed that the only way to secure voting rights for women was to institutionalize the prohibition of alcohol

(B) Frances Willard believed that securing voting rights for women was to institutionalize the prohibition of alcohol as the only way

(C) voting rights for women were secured by Frances Willard's belief in institutionalizing the prohibition of alcohol

(D) women believed their voting rights could be secured by Frances Willard's prohibition of alcohol

(E) Frances Willard, having believed in institutionalizing the prohibition of alcohol, securing voting rights for women

14. Earning good money with only a bachelor's degree can be very difficult, since current standards of living usually require more <u>income, this being the reason for many college graduates to continue pursuing higher education.</u>

(A) income, this being the reason for many college graduates to continue pursuing higher education

(B) income explaining the continued pursuit for higher education by college graduates

(C) income; this reason being why many college graduates continue the pursuit for higher education

(D) income; and for this reason, many college graduates continue to pursue higher education

(E) income; this is the reason that many college graduates continue to pursue higher education

STOP
**If you finish before time is called, you may check your work on this section only.
Do not turn to any other section in the test.**

(ANSWERS ON PAGE 208)

Chapter 16
PRACTICE TEST 2

SECTION 1
Time–25 minutes
35 Questions

1. The farmer decided, after long deliberation, that the best course of action would include spreading the soil, replacing the crops, and <u>the irrigation canal should be shifted</u>.

   (A) the irrigation canal should be shifted
   (B) would include shifting the irrigation canal
   (C) shifting the irrigation canal
   (D) the irrigation canal must be shifted
   (E) should irrigate the canal by shifting

2. When he left the stadium, <u>Charles, looking back one last time</u> and couldn't believe that this time-honored structure would be razed despite the recent preservation efforts.

   (A) Charles, looking back one last time
   (B) Charles looked back one last time
   (C) Charles would have looked one last time
   (D) Charles, for the last time, having looked back
   (E) Charles, for the last time, looks back

3. The doctoral candidates were accomplished professionals in their fields, groundbreaking innovators in their disciplines, and, <u>most importantly, have a natural teaching ability in a lecture hall</u>.

   (A) most importantly, have a natural teaching ability in a lecture hall
   (B) more importantly, natural teachers in a lecture hall
   (C) most importantly, natural teachers in the lecture hall
   (D) most importantly, the ability to teach naturally in a lecture hall
   (E) more importantly, has a natural teaching ability in a lecture hall

4. One in every five adults above the age of twenty <u>suffer from chronic sleep deprivation, which leads to unintended weight gain</u> because of improper eating habits.

   (A) suffer from chronic sleep deprivation, which leads to unintended weight gain
   (B) suffer from chronic sleep deprivation, which led to unintended weight gain
   (C) will suffer from chronic sleep deprivation, which, has led to unintended weight gain
   (D) were suffering from chronic sleep deprivation, which leads to unintended weight gain
   (E) suffers from chronic sleep deprivation, which leads to unintended weight gain

5. <u>The ocean bottom having been explored</u>, the diver was intrigued to discover the remains of a prehistoric organism once thought to be extinct.

   (A) The ocean bottom having been explored
   (B) The bottom of the ocean being explored
   (C) When having explored the ocean's bottom
   (D) When she explored the ocean's bottom
   (E) She explored the bottom of the ocean

6. In 2010, Kathryn Bigelow became the first woman to win an Academy Award for film direction, <u>but there has been neither a female winner or a nominee since then</u>.

   (A) but there has been neither a female winner or a nominee since then
   (B) but there has been neither a female winner nor a female nominee since then
   (C) and since then, there has been either a winner or a female nominee
   (D) there was neither female winners nor female nominees since then
   (E) there has been, since then, neither a female winner nor a female nominee

7. The photographer and the producer, who had recently been embroiled in a major copyright dispute, have nonetheless reunited to create an installation for an art museum in San Diego.

(A) in a major copyright dispute, have nonetheless reunited

(B) in a major copyright dispute, has reunited nonetheless

(C) and had a major copyright dispute, which reuniting them nonetheless

(D) and had disputed a major copyright, they have nonetheless reunited

(E) in disputing, they reunited and nonetheless had a major copyright

8. Prior to the Hispanicization of the Philippines, the social roles of women go beyond the traditional domestic expectations and included community leadership through shamanism.

(A) the social roles of women go beyond the traditional domestic expectations

(B) women's social roles went beyond the traditional domestic expectations

(C) the social roles of women goes far beyond the traditional domestic expectations

(D) women's traditional domestic expectations go beyond that of their social roles

(E) the traditional domestic expectations have been going from the social roles of women

9. Reputable cinematographer and filmmaker Gordon Willis, who was known for his work on such films as *The Godfather* and *Annie Hall*, but one subject of a recent documentary on legendary Hollywood figures.

(A) but

(B) having been

(C) also would become

(D) is

(E) but being

10. A legendary singer, songwriter, and civil rights activist, the prestigious Curtis Institute in Philadelphia rejected Nina Simone despite a perfect piano audition.

(A) the prestigious Curtis Institute in Philadelphia rejected Nina Simone

(B) the prestigious Curtis Institute in Philadelphia will reject Nina Simone

(C) Nina Simone, having been rejected by the prestigious Curtis Institute in Philadelphia

(D) Nina Simone's rejection from the prestigious Curtis Institute in Philadelphia

(E) Nina Simone was rejected by the prestigious Curtis Institute in Philadelphia

11. José Rizal, who has been compared to Martin Luther King, published several works that mocked the foundations of Western civility, despite him once believing that the Philippines will have amicable Western relations.

(A) despite him once believing that the Philippines will have amicable Western relations

(B) even though he once believed that the Philippines could have amicable relations with the West

(C) although he would have believed that the Philippines could have amicable Western relations

(D) and once believing that the Philippines could have amicable Western relations

(E) and the Philippines, he believed, could have amicable Western relations

16   16   16   16   16   16   16

Unauthorized copying or reuse of any part of this page is illegal.

Practice Test 2

12. Mrs. Carroway's accusation that Reginald

had plagiarized from her novel being baseless,
    A   B

since the copyright date of his work predated
C

that of her own. No error
    D   E

13. Laura asked Richard if he would please sit
                  A

quiet on the sofa until the doctor arrived to perform
B   C   D

his medical diagnosis. No error
          E

14. With its developed storyline and unique setting,
  A

Gail's television pilot drew more attention from
                B

the producers at the meeting than did Jonathan.
          C   D

No error
E

15. Although there are many renditions of
    A

Shakespeare's plays, a few cutting-edge

performances recently has featured exclusively
      B   C   D

male casts. No error
     E

16. It is widely maintained that the pig is an
        A   B

extremely intelligent animal, it is capable of
                C

solving mathematical problems even more

efficiently than either a dog or a trained bear can.
     D

No error
E

17. Without so much as a sigh, the little boy endured
      A   B

the pain from the stitches holding his mother's
     C   D

hand. No error
E

18. All employees above the age of sixty-five who
       A

were grandfathered into the new company before
     B

the merger was able to retain their retirement
     C   D

benefits despite the new policy. No error
       E

19. Between Jonathan, Sarah, and Zachary, Sarah earned
    A

the highest score on the astronautics exam
    B   C

because of her ability to withstand high amounts
         D

of stress. No error
     E

20. The octopus can change their shape and color to
          A

camouflage with the environment both in an effort
      B   C

to catch unsuspecting prey and to avoid predators.
        D

No error
E

21. His careful attention to detail and his unrelenting
         A   B

endurance has improved the quality and condition
     C

of the magazine's articles. No error
    D   E

Practice Test 2

22. Gretchen, although weary from her travels,

    hiked <u>for a week</u>, made camp on the last day,
          A

    and <u>she found</u> her way home by following a path
        B

    <u>along the south</u> side of <u>the valley</u>. <u>No error</u>
         C   D   E

23. The university student <u>presented</u> a
                            A

    <u>particularly innovative</u> thesis project, an artificially
         B

    intelligent painting machine <u>that creates its own</u>
                                  C

    artwork when <u>entering Boolean algebra</u>. <u>No error</u>
                      D   E

24. The committee decided that <u>its</u> best <u>course of</u>
                               A   B

    action would be <u>to suspend</u> the candidate search
                    C

    and wait for the appearance of a <u>more qualified</u> set
                                      D

    of applicants. <u>No error</u>
                   E

25. Before the insurgency could enact <u>their</u> covert plan
                                      A

    to overthrow the establishment that <u>had been run</u>
                                         B

    by the military dictator, innocent civilians had lost

    <u>their homes</u> and families <u>to</u> amoral policies.
        C   D

    <u>No error</u>
    E

26. <u>Although</u> often surrounded by scandal
    A

    <u>in his lifetime,</u> Gustave Flaubert <u>is remembered</u>
        B   C

    today not for his fraught personal life <u>but for</u> his
                                             D

    prose masterpiece *Madame Bovary*. <u>No error</u>
                                         E

27. Mr. Tsong's international restaurant <u>has made</u>
                                        A

    a name <u>for itself</u> with dishes that combine
           B

    ingredients from very different cultures, <u>such as</u>
                                               C

    pizzas topped with marinated cactus and tacos

    <u>garnished to</u> Asian baby carrots. <u>No error</u>
        D   E

28. Senator Grosvenor's son <u>addressed</u> the crowd
                            A

    and announced that <u>his father</u> would not be
                       B

    seeking re-election, much <u>to the dismay</u> of
                              C

    the loyal voters <u>who had flocked</u> to hear the
                     D

    young man speak. <u>No error</u>
                     E

29. Because <u>there is</u> no financial reward
            A

    <u>for completing</u> the United States census, many
        B

    citizens <u>feel that they</u> have <u>less reasons</u> than
             C   D

    ever before to spend valuable time filling in

    census forms. <u>No error</u>
                   E

Practice Test 2

(1) For many, the greatest Japanese filmmaker isn't a man who makes blockbusters or sci-fi epics, like George Lucas or Steven Spielberg. (2) Instead, Japan's greatest director is Yasujiro Ozu, the creator of very different, much more down-to-earth movies. (3) What is the typical Ozu movie like? (4) Very often, the film starts with a family or other small group of people dealing with everyday problems. (5) By the end, things have often changed, with maybe a marriage or travel plans or a new friendship being formed. (6) This is the usual extent of what Ozu has for the plot, and the camera shots are always very simple and direct, completely free of confusion.

(7) Why is Ozu so astonishing? (8) There are a few great answers to this question, the first is that Ozu's films are about fascinating moments in history. (9) Between 1920 and 1960, when Ozu was very active, Japan and its people wanted to modernize themselves yet also prized their cultural traditions. (10) This tension between old and new makes his work fascinating. (11) The other main reason is that Ozu is a great storyteller. (12) In his film *Tokyo Story*, for instance, he tells how two aging parents visit their children. (13) From the old father and mother down to their grandchildren, all the characters in *Tokyo Story* are depicted with a combination of gentle humor and compassion.

30. What is the best way to deal with sentence 1?

(A) Leave it as it is.
(B) Add the word "do" after "Steven Spielberg".
(C) Change "many" to "most people".
(D) Insert the word "either" immediately before "blockbusters or sci-fi epics".
(E) Insert the phrase "oddly enough" at the beginning of the sentence.

31. To improve the structure of the essay, what should be done with sentence 3?

(A) Leave it as it is.
(B) Remove the sentence.
(C) Insert it after sentence 1.
(D) Insert it before sentence 6.
(E) Change "movie" to "story".

32. Which of the following revisions would most improve sentence 6?

(A) Insert "Nevertheless" at the beginning.
(B) Change "This" to "That".
(C) Change "and" to "however".
(D) Add "not" before "usual".
(E) Change "what Ozu has for the plot" to "the plot".

33. Which of the following changes to sentence 8 is the most necessary?

(A) Insert "exsist" after "question".
(B) Change "few" to "less".
(C) Replace the comma with a colon.
(D) Change "are a few" to "were some".
(E) Replace the comma with "but".

34. What is the best way to revise the underlined portion of sentence 9 (reproduced below)?

Between 1920 and 1960, when Ozu was very active, Japan and its people wanted to modernize themselves yet also prized their cultural traditions.

(A) (As it is now)
(B) the Japanese wanted to modernize their country yet also prized their cultural traditions
(C) Japan wanted to modernize itself, and also prized cultural traditions
(D) the Japanese wanted to modernize, but wanted to prize cultural traditions also
(E) the Japanese wanted their country modernized yet also have prized its cultural traditions

35. Which of the following, if placed after sentence 13, would be the most effective concluding sentence for the essay?

(A) Ozu was also fascinated by the artistic possibilities that Technicolor films offered, even though Ozu masterpieces such as *Tokyo Story* were shot in black-and-white.

(B) It is possible, nonetheless, to criticize *Tokyo Story* for only touching lightly on the economic hardships that many Japanese citizens experienced in Ozu's day.

(C) Like Ozu, current day filmmaker Ang Lee considers important cultural and social themes, thus validating Ozu's impact within the independent film industry.

(D) By turning a sympathetic eye on the different generations in a fast-transforming Japan, Ozu was able to craft films that are uniquely twentieth-century works of art.

(E) Nevertheless, Ozu's artistic vision was limited by the overbearing influence of European storytelling techniques.

STOP
If you finish before time is called, you may check your work on this section only.
Do not turn to any other section in the test.

SECTION 2
Time–10 minutes
14 Questions

1. <u>Compared from</u> his prim and reserved contemporary Samuel Richardson, novelist Henry Fielding lived a life distinguished by sensual indulgences and daring political disputes.

   (A) Compared from
   (B) Compared against
   (C) Unlike
   (D) Unlike from
   (E) Unlike to

2. Chelsea succeeded as an actress not only because of her remarkable poise <u>but also because of being able for her to depict convincingly a range of characters.</u>

   (A) but also because of being able for her to depict convincingly a range of characters
   (B) but also because of her ability to convincingly depict a range of characters
   (C) and also from her ability to depict a range of characters convincingly
   (D) yet she was also able to convincingly depict a range of characters
   (E) however, she succeeded in addition to her convincing depiction of a range of characters

3. Professor Jimenez acknowledges that metaphysics is a difficult subject to present to a college class; fortunately, <u>it is explained clearly in her new book, where there are employed</u> straightforward analogies to elucidate challenging concepts.

   (A) it is explained clearly in her new book, where there are employed
   (B) they are clearly explained in her new book, which employed
   (C) metaphysics is clearly explained in her new book, which employs
   (D) she has explained metaphysics in her new book, yet it employs
   (E) metaphysics is the explanation from her new book, employing

4. A recent article entitled "The Decline and Fall of the Modern History Department" makes the provocative claim that too many contemporary historians <u>are replacing disciplined archival research with making speculations in ways that are irresponsible</u>.

   (A) are replacing disciplined archival research with making speculations in ways that are irresponsible
   (B) are replacing disciplined archival research with irresponsible speculation
   (C) had been replacing archival research with discipline against speculation from irresponsibility
   (D) are replaced by disciplined archival research from irresponsible speculation
   (E) replace research with discipline from irresponsibility and speculation

5. He had expected to finish his doctoral degree in four years at most, <u>but instead he studies for almost a decade and only earned his diploma a few years ago, at thirty-seven years old</u>.

   (A) but instead he studies for almost a decade and only earned his diploma a few years ago, at thirty-seven years old
   (B) but instead after studying for almost a decade and only earning his diploma a few years ago, when he was thirty-seven years old
   (C) however, by studying for almost a decade, he will earn his diploma only a few years ago, when he will be thirty-seven years old
   (D) but he studied for almost a decade; now, earning his diploma a few years ago, at thirty-seven years old
   (E) but instead he studied for almost a decade and only earned his diploma a few years ago, when he was thirty-seven years old

6. On account of her ability to recall even minute pieces of evidence with little study, <u>Olivia's teachers labeled her a student with a photographic memory</u>.

(A) Olivia's teachers labeled her a student with a photographic memory
(B) Olivia has been labeled a student with a photographic memory by her teachers
(C) Olivia's teachers are labeling her a student whose memory is photographic
(D) Olivia is a student with a memory, which is the photographic label from her teachers
(E) Olivia's memory has been labeled photographic by her teachers

7. Once belittled as childish and unintelligent "doodles," <u>Cy Twombly and Jean-Michel Basquiat are artists who have elevated playful, carefree sketches to a respected form of self-expression</u>.

(A) Cy Twombly and Jean-Michel Basquiat are artists who have elevated playful, carefree sketches to a respected form of self-expression
(B) a respected form of self expression has been elevated from playful, carefree sketches by artists such as Cy Twombly and Jean-Michel Basquiat
(C) sketches that are playful and carefree had elevated artists such as Cy Twombly and Jean-Michel Basquiat into a respected form of self-expression
(D) playful and carefree sketches have been elevated to a respected form of self-expression by artists such as Cy Twombly and Jean-Michel Basquiat
(E) playful and carefree sketches were elevated into a respected form of self-expression; Jean-Michel Basquiat and Cy Twombly being two artists who did this

8. The butterfly habitat is one of the most popular attractions at the Bronx Zoo, even though <u>there are strict rules for the exhibit, making it difficult from access by stroller or wheelchair</u>.

(A) there are strict rules for the exhibit, making it difficult from access by stroller or wheelchair
(B) there are strict rules in the exhibit, which are difficult for access by stroller or wheelchair
(C) there are strict rules, for which the exhibit being difficult by access from stroller or wheelchair
(D) there are strict rules that make it difficult to access the exhibit by stroller or wheelchair
(E) there is strict rules for the exhibit that make access by stroller and wheelchair difficult

9. <u>Absented from both having strong leaders and any meaningful principle of cooperation</u>, the members of the faculty committee succumbed to petty squabbles that made productive discussion impossible.

(A) Absented from both having strong leaders and any meaningful principle of cooperation
(B) From the absence of strong leadership or cooperating with meaningful principles
(C) In the absence of both strong leaders and any meaningful principle of cooperation
(D) In the absence of either strong leaders, but also meaningful cooperation principles
(E) In the absence of strong leaders, and meaningful principles were also absent from cooperation

10. Intrigued by the glories of the long-vanished Inca Empire, Victor has arranged a trip to Peru, <u>where the ruins of Inca houses and roadways can still be visited by tourists</u>.

(A) where the ruins of Inca houses and roadways can still be visited by tourists
(B) in which tourists are still visiting the ruins of Inca houses and also roadways
(C) from where the ruins of Inca houses and roadways had been visited among tourists
(D) when tourists can still have been visiting the ruins of Inca houses, roadways as well
(E) in which tourists can still make visits to both Inca houses as well as its roadways

11. At first, <u>Sylvia looked ridiculous on a sunny day and she carried a large black golf umbrella</u>; around noon, however, a sudden burst of rain allowed her to put her possession to good use.

(A) Sylvia looked ridiculous on a sunny day and she carried a large black golf umbrella
(B) Sylvia looking ridiculous on a sunny day, carrying a large black golf umbrella
(C) Sylvia, looking ridiculous, had carried by a sunny day and large black golf umbrella
(D) Sylvia had carried a large black golf umbrella on a sunny day to be looking ridiculous
(E) Sylvia looked ridiculous carrying a large black golf umbrella on a sunny day

Practice Test 2

12. Attempts to simplify the spelling conventions of the English language are often derided by teachers and students alike; it is hard to imagine many school communities willingly changing the spelling of "tough" to "tuff."

(A) Attempts to simplify the spelling conventions of the English language are often derided by teachers and students alike; it is hard to imagine

(B) Attempts to simplify the spelling conventions of the English language are often derided by teachers and students alike; they are hard to imagine

(C) Attempts to simplify the spelling conventions of the English language being derided against teachers and students alike, it is hard to imagine

(D) Attempts which simplify the spelling conventions of the English language often derided by teachers and students alike, they are hard to imagine

(E) To simplify the spelling conventions of the English language, which are often derided by teachers and students alike, it would be hard to imagine

13. Because the lunar moth is one of the largest airborne insects, its wings sometimes stretch to four inches across.

(A) Because the lunar moth is one of the largest airborne insects, its wings sometimes stretch to four inches across.

(B) The lunar moth is one of the largest airborne insects, its wings sometimes stretch to four inches across.

(C) With its wings sometimes stretching four inches across, the lunar moths are one of the largest airborne insects.

(D) Their wings sometimes stretching four inches across, the lunar moth is one of the largest airborne insects

(E) The lunar moth is one of the largest airborne insects; its wings sometimes stretch four inches across.

14. People with high levels of confidence are driven to succeed, but are not necessarily good at managing their time; even the most confident being known to leave obligations to the last minute.

(A) but are not necessarily good at managing their time; even the most confident being known to and leave obligations to the last minute

(B) not necessarily however good at managing their time; even the most confident are known to leave obligations as in the last minute

(C) but are not necessarily good at managing their time; even the most confident of these individuals are known to leave obligations to the last minute

(D) however, they were not necessarily good at managing time; even the most confident of them had been known to leave obligations to the last minute

(E) but it is not necessarily good for these individuals when managing time; even the most confident are leaving obligations to the last minute

STOP
If you finish before time is called, you may check your work on this section only.
Do not turn to any other section in the test.

Chapter 17
PRACTICE TEST 3

SECTION 1
Time–25 minutes
35 Questions

1. Whether an activist works on environmental, social, or economic issues, <u>dedication</u> to the cause is vital for success.

   (A) dedication
   (B) he or she, while dedicating
   (C) by dedicating
   (D) through having dedication
   (E) they need to have dedication

2. The lessons one learns from past mistakes <u>helps one to avoid</u> future blunders.

   (A) helps one to avoid
   (B) helps you to avoid
   (C) help one to avoid
   (D) help you in the act of avoiding
   (E) help them to avoid

3. An influential American painter, Barnett Newman created numerous <u>masterpieces, which he also invented</u> a unique style of "color field" painting.

   (A) masterpieces, which he also invented
   (B) masterpieces, he also invented
   (C) masterpieces and invented
   (D) masterpieces, even more impressive, he invented
   (E) masterpieces, also being the inventor of

4. When the president was inaugurated, he promised to protect the people of the country with good diplomacy and a strong military, <u>and to foster</u> the growth of the domestic economy.

   (A) and to foster
   (B) and fostering
   (C) and it is fostering
   (D) and fostered
   (E) and his promise was he would foster

5. <u>By growing fresh produce</u> on vacant lots in urban areas will decrease crime in blighted neighborhoods and provide locals with access to healthy and affordable food.

   (A) By growing fresh produce
   (B) Growing fresh produce
   (C) If we start to grow fresh produce
   (D) Because growing fresh produce
   (E) To have grown fresh produce

6. Marina Abromović, a modern day performance artist who enjoys international fame, <u>sometimes invites</u> her audience to help to create her artwork.

   (A) sometimes invites
   (B) sometimes inviting
   (C) who sometimes invites
   (D) she sometimes invites
   (E) sometimes invited

7. In 1991, Michael J. Fox, a Canadian-American actor, <u>was diagnosed with Parkinson's disease, it is a degenerative disorder that affects</u> the central nervous system.

   (A) was diagnosed with Parkinson's disease, it is a degenerative disorder that affects
   (B) being diagnosed with Parkinson's disease, a degenerative disorder that affects
   (C) is diagnosed with Parkinson's disease, it is a degenerative disorder that affects
   (D) who was diagnosed with Parkinson's disease, a degenerative disorder that affects
   (E) was diagnosed with Parkinson's disease, a degenerative disorder that affects

Practice Test 3

8. Paula, who is now making reservations at an Italian restaurant for her blind date on Saturday, <u>and nervously anticipating the prospect of meeting her future husband</u>.

   (A) and nervously anticipating the prospect of meeting her future husband
   (B) and nervously anticipates the prospect of meeting her future husband
   (C) because she nervously anticipates the prospect of meeting her future husband
   (D) nervously anticipates the prospect of meeting her future husband
   (E) she nervously anticipates the prospect of meeting her future husband

9. The recently completed washing and repainting <u>has turned</u> the previously dilapidated house into a desirable property.

   (A) has turned
   (B) turning
   (C) would be turning
   (D) have turned
   (E) turns

10. Bonnie Parker and Clyde Barrow, <u>infamous outlaws from the Great Depression era, made a living as traveling bank robbers in Louisiana until 1934,</u> where they were finally ambushed and shot dead.

   (A) infamous outlaws from the Great Depression era, made a living as traveling bank robbers in Louisiana until 1934
   (B) infamous outlaws from the Great Depression era, made a living as traveling bank robbers until 1934 in Louisiana
   (C) infamous outlaws in Louisiana from the Great Depression era, made a living as traveling bank robbers until 1934
   (D) infamous outlaws from the Great Depression era, made a living as a traveling bank robber until 1934
   (E) infamous outlaws from the Great Depression era, making a living as traveling bank robbers until 1934 in Louisiana

11. <u>Raphael tweaked the muffin recipe, which normally required massive amounts of butter and sugar, in the hope of convincing</u> Sarah to indulge in his pastries despite her new diet.

   (A) Raphael tweaked the muffin recipe, which normally required massive amounts of butter and sugar, in the hope of convincing
   (B) Normally requiring massive amounts of sugar and butter, Raphael tweaked the muffin recipe, hoping to convince
   (C) The muffin recipe, normally requiring massive amounts of sugar and butter, was tweaked by Raphael, despite this hoping to convince
   (D) Raphael, normally requiring massive amounts of sugar and butter, tweaked the muffin recipe, hoping he would convince
   (E) Raphael tweaked the muffin recipe, which normally required massive amounts of sugar and butter, yet he hoped he would convince

12. <u>Critics attacked</u> the new theatrical adaptation of
      A

John Steinbeck's *The Grapes of Wrath*, <u>which</u> they
                                   B

accused of <u>sugarcoated</u> the <u>most challenging</u>
            C   D

social themes in Steinbeck's novel. <u>No error</u>
                           E

13. <u>During</u> the 1970s, <u>the films of</u> Woody Allen
    A   B

<u>establishing</u> a new pop-culture icon, the
    C

<u>self-consciously</u> "uncool" Manhattan intellectual,
        D

in the American imagination. <u>No error</u>
                   E

14. Both sand and sand flies <u>make</u> visiting the beach
                  A

<u>a bit of</u> an uncomfortable experience, but
    B

<u>it also provides</u> humans with a better understanding
    C

<u>of</u> the cruelty of mother nature. <u>No error</u>
D   E

15. <u>There</u> are many children who dream of
    A

becoming movie stars, but the real probability of

achieving celebrity status <u>is</u> very slim and several
                  B

of <u>these adolescents</u> will grow up to be little more
    C

than <u>a disappointed dreamer</u>. <u>No error</u>
       D   E

16. <u>Ever since she</u> was a teenager, Mary <u>is leaving</u>
      A   B

her keys and wallet in the house every time she

sets out to go somewhere; <u>her</u> forgetfulness
               C

continues to <u>drive everyone</u> crazy. <u>No error</u>
         D   E

17. Before he decided to go to college, Mark <u>spent</u>
                          A

several years working in restaurants and shops

<u>where</u> the demand for disciplined behavior
    B

<u>was</u> commonly instilled in <u>every</u> worker. <u>No error</u>
C   D   E

18. Instead of <u>complaining incessantly</u> about your
            A

<u>problems at</u> work, <u>one could</u> take proactive steps
    B   C

and begin writing a newsletter to foster

better on-the-job <u>environments</u>. <u>No error</u>
              D   E

19. The National September 11 Memorial and Museum

<u>provides</u> a peaceful place not only for families
    A

<u>mourning</u> deceased loved ones <u>and also</u> for
    B   C

everyday citizens interested in learning about the

<u>efforts of</u> first responders. <u>No error</u>
    D   E

20. <u>That</u> the artists <u>were unable</u> to sell the landscapes
    A   B

and watercolors that they <u>had created</u> at the recent
                  C

retreat suggests that the market for traditional

painting <u>is shrinking</u>. <u>No error</u>
      D   E

21. Recently, sales of candy <u>has been</u> bolstered by an
                  A

unconventional <u>yet much-publicized</u> study of the
           B

many health benefits <u>of eating</u> chocolate, peanuts,
            C

<u>and</u> certain varieties of caramel. <u>No error</u>
D   E

22. The capybara is <u>the largest rodent</u> currently living;
                        A

when some tourists encounter this enormous

mammal for the first time, they mistake <u>them</u> for
                                          B

<u>either</u> a bear <u>or a pony</u>. <u>No error</u>
  C   D   E

23. Literary scholars <u>argue that</u> John Milton's *Paradise*
                   A

Lost <u>contains</u> a network <u>of illusions</u> to earlier texts
        B   C

and poems, including the plays of Shakespeare

<u>and the Bible</u>. <u>No error</u>
    D   E

24. The telecommunication company makes a point

<u>of giving</u> all <u>perspective</u> employees guided tours
  A   B

of the facilities, <u>even though</u> only a few of
               C

<u>these candidates</u> receive formal interview offers.
    D

<u>No error</u>
  E

25. Visitors to Mecca, <u>which is</u> perhaps the most
                A

important holy city of Islam, <u>braves</u> desert heat
                 B

and crowds <u>of pilgrims</u> in order to reach
          C

<u>the revered landmarks</u> of this metropolis. <u>No error</u>
      D   E

26. The interior <u>decorator encouraged</u> me to buy chairs
              A

and sofas <u>in burgundy</u> or dark green, <u>but</u> I am
        B   C

<u>particular to</u> lighter colors such as sky blue and
     D

lemon yellow. <u>No error</u>
        E

27. <u>Dressed as</u> superheroes such as Wonder Woman and
    A

Aqua Man, <u>the members</u> of the anti-bullying
        B

organization <u>visited</u> the grammar school
        C

<u>speaking about</u> good social values. <u>No error</u>
    D   E

28. Convinced that the evidence of wrongdoing

<u>was tenuous</u> at best, the jury <u>delivered</u> a resounding
  A   B

verdict of "not guilty," thus <u>freeing</u> the accused
                  C

parties of all charges <u>of embezzlement</u>. <u>No error</u>
              D   E

29. Though reviled <u>of many early listeners</u>, musical
              A

genres <u>such as</u> rap and hip-hop <u>are becoming</u>
      B   C

increasingly respected <u>as forms of</u> art that comment
               D

on important social problems. <u>No error</u>
              E

17 17 17 17 17 17 17

Unauthorized copying or reuse of any part of this page is illegal.

(1) By working together, a hardy group of pet enthusiasts has created a community organization with the potential to do an enormous amount of good. (2) In 2007, People Pick-Me-Up began when two young schoolteachers began bringing their pets—rabbits, parakeets, even a cheerful golden retriever—to a local nursing home. (3) The idea of using visiting pets to comfort others quickly caught on, with now People Pick-Me-Up boasting over twenty active members and recognition in a large number of local and state newspapers. (4) The group's portfolio of regular visit locations include everything from nursing homes to veterans' hospitals to camps for children from troubled families.

(5) The key to the success of People Pick-Me-Up has been its dedication to the immediate community: in this case, a few counties in suburban Connecticut. (6) "We have had plenty of opportunities to expand, but we would rather build stronger connections to the people we know," says Ron MacKinner, one of the two People Pick-Me-Up founding members. (7) However, MacKinner doesn't see this local emphasis as turning his back on people in need. (8) He hopes that other organizations will see the good work People Pick-Me-Up is doing and follow its example. (9) MacKinner's own background is in management and entrepreneurship, both of which he studied at the university level.

(10) In the end, this "inspire others far and wide" strategy has begun to show positive results. (11) Other pet therapy groups have begun to follow the approach set by MacKinner, and one newly-established organization in rural Pennsylvania even cites the good work done by People Pick-Me-Up as its specific inspiration.

30. In context, what is the best way to deal with sentence 1?

    (A) Leave it as it is.
    (B) Change "has" to "have".
    (C) Change "enormous" to "more enormous".
    (D) Change "to do" to "of doing".
    (E) Change "By working together" to "For working together".

31. Which of the following is the best way to revise the underlined portion of sentence 3 (reproduced below)?

    The idea of using visiting pets to comfort others quickly caught on, with now People Pick-Me-Up boasting over twenty active members and recognition in a large number of local and state newspapers.

    (A) quickly caught on; now, People Pick-Me-Up boasting
    (B) quickly it caught on; People Pick-Me-Up boasts now
    (C) quickly caught on; now, People Pick-Me-Up boasts
    (D) quickly caught on, because People Pick-Me-Up now boasts
    (E) quickly caught on, even though People Pick-Me-Up now can boast

32. Which of the corrections below is most necessary for sentence 4?

    (A) Change "visit locations" to "visits".
    (B) Change "include" to "includes".
    (C) Delete the phrase "everything from".
    (D) Delete the phrase "from troubled families".
    (E) Insert the word "Consequently" at the beginning of the sentence.

33. What would be best to do with sentence 9?

    (A) Use "even though" to combine it with sentence 8.
    (B) Move it to the end of the first paragraph.
    (C) Move it to the beginning of the third paragraph.
    (D) Move it to the end of the third paragraph.
    (E) Delete it from the passage.

34. In context, which of the following phrases could replace "In the end" at the beginning of sentence 10?

(A) Despite this
(B) However
(C) Oddly enough
(D) Recently
(E) Finally

35. Which of the following would be the most effective concluding sentence for the passage?

(A) It is possible that MaKinner's philosophy of locally-oriented community service was a product of his college years, when he was employed by a start-up company that provided gift baskets for the elderly.

(B) In another respect, though, this growth is surprising, since rural Pennsylvania has few nursing homes compared to Philadelphia and its suburbs.

(C) MacKinner's vision of community service that stays local yet influences far and wide is well on its way to becoming a reality.

(D) MacKinner has also received letters of interest, a few of which make reference to People Pick-Me-Up, from just a little beyond his own area of Connecticut.

(E) While nursing home visits make up the vast majority of the activities of People Pick-Me-Up, the group has scheduled several events at daycare centers for the summer ahead.

STOP
If you finish before time is called, you may check your work on this section only.
Do not turn to any other section in the test.

SECTION 2
Time–10 minutes
14 Questions

1. <u>Ringo Starr is widely regarded as the least influential member of the Beatles,</u> he in fact created some highly innovative songs and melodies.

   (A) Ringo Starr is widely regarded as the least influential member of the Beatles
   (B) Since Ringo Starr widely regarded as the least influential member of the Beatles
   (C) Although Ringo Starr is widely regarded as the least influential member of the Beatles
   (D) Ringo Starr, despite being widely regarded as the least influential member of the Beatles
   (E) In contrast to the fact that Ringo Starr is widely regarded as the least influential member of the Beatles

2. While clothing designers located in New York have historically been <u>more successful than the Midwest,</u> a new group of Chicago-based fashion entrepreneurs is beginning to capture the attention of the media.

   (A) more successful than the Midwest
   (B) more successful than designers in the Midwest
   (C) most successful compared to the Midwest
   (D) more successful unlike Midwest designers
   (E) more successful from those in the Midwest

3. In the 1950s, linguists and biologists were firmly convinced that chimpanzees lack any true understanding of language concepts; <u>since then, however, new research emerging proving they can recognize fundamental nouns and verbs.</u>

   (A) since then, however, new research emerging proving they can recognize fundamental nouns and verbs
   (B) since then, however, the emergence of new research on chimpanzees proving they are recognizing fundamental nouns and verbs
   (C) since then, however, new research has emerged which proves that chimpanzees can recognize fundamental nouns and verbs
   (D) however, research which have emerged since then on chimpanzees prove they can recognize fundamental nous and verbs
   (E) yet new research will emerge since then, because it is proving that chimpanzees can recognize fundamental nouns and verbs

4. After climbing a mountain like Everest all the way to its summit, you experience a sensation that <u>feels wonderful, overwhelming, and it can feel frightening.</u>

   (A) feels wonderful, overwhelming, and it can feel frightening
   (B) feels wonderful, overwhelming, and even frightening
   (C) feeling wonderful, overwhelming, and frightening
   (D) feel wonderful, overwhelming, and frightening to some people
   (E) feels wonderful, overwhelming, also frightening

5. Using three-dimensional image modeling technology and plastic materials, <u>prosthetic limbs have been created by professionals that are affordable and comfortable for patients.</u>

   (A) prosthetic limbs have been created by professionals that are affordable and comfortable for patients
   (B) affordable and comfortable for patients, are prosthetic limbs created by professionals
   (C) prosthetic limbs that are affordable and comfortable for patients have been created by professionals
   (D) professionals have created prosthetic limbs that are affordable and comfortable for patients
   (E) professionals, affordable and comfortable, have created prosthetic limbs for patients

6. In 2009, for his efforts to strengthen diplomatic cooperation, Barack Obama won the Nobel Peace Prize, <u>which he was the fourth United States president to receive that honor.</u>

   (A) which he was the fourth United States president to receive that honor
   (B) he was the fourth United States president to receive that honor
   (C) becoming the fourth United States president to receive that honor
   (D) the fourth United States president receiving that honor
   (E) receiving that honor as the fourth United States president

7. To avoid doing his homework, Jason offered to help his mother around the house by vacuuming the stairs, dusted the windowsills, and mowing the lawn.

(A) house by vacuuming the stairs, dusted the windowsills, and mowing
(B) house; vacuuming the stairs, dusting the windowsills, and mowing
(C) house, he vacuumed the stairs, dusted the windowsills, and mowed
(D) house by vacuuming the stairs, dusting the windowsills, and mowing
(E) house, he vacuumed the stairs, dusting the windowsills and mowing

8. Suspension bridges, like San Francisco's Golden Gate Bridge, support roadways as long as 7,000 feet by connecting weight-bearing towers to numerous cables or chains.

(A) support roadways as long as 7,000 feet by connecting
(B) supports roadways as long as 7,000 feet by connecting
(C) support roadways as long as 7,000 feet, they connect
(D) they support roadways as long as 7,000 feet by connecting
(E) by supporting roadways as long as 7,000 feet and connecting

9. Billy Holiday's song "Strange Fruit", despite it being a song ostensibly about unusual produce, is a critique of American racism and violent crimes against African-Americans.

(A) despite it being a song
(B) though
(C) it is a song
(D) in addition to being
(E) irregardless of being

10. Janice is so desperate to be accepted by her peers, therefore, she conforms to modes of behavior that she thinks will make her look cool.

(A) peers, therefore, she conforms
(B) peers, conforming
(C) peers in that she conforms
(D) peers, thus conforming
(E) peers that she conforms

11. In his celebrated play *Who's Afraid of Virginia Woolf?*, Edward Albee, by focusing on just two volatile marriages, to set forth a larger statement about unhappiness and discontent in 1960s America.

(A) Edward Albee, by focusing on just two volatile marriages, to set forth a larger statement about unhappiness and discontent in 1960s America
(B) Edward Albee sets forth a larger statement about unhappiness and discontent in 1960s America, which focuses on just two volatile marriages
(C) Edward Albee focused on just two volatile marriages and sets forth a larger statement about unhappiness and discontent in 1960s America
(D) Edward Albee, by focusing on just two volatile marriages, set forth a larger statement about unhappiness and discontent in 1960s America
(E) Edward Albee focused on just two volatile marriages, and because of this setting forth a larger statement about unhappiness and discontent in 1960s America

12. Although he prepares for the marathon for over three months, Xavier is still not certain that he has built up enough stamina to make it through all 25 miles of the race.

(A) Although he prepares for the marathon for over three months
(B) From preparing for over three months for the marathon
(C) Although he has prepared for the marathon for over three months
(D) While preparing for the marathon for over three months
(E) Although he prepared for the marathon, despite it being over three months

135

17 17 17 17 17 17 17

Unauthorized copying or reuse of any part of this page is illegal.

13. Recently, a large number of investigative journalists have criticized the chemical and agricultural company Monsanto, these writers are especially critical of the company's policies regarding genetically modified seeds.

   (A) the chemical and agricultural company Monsanto, these writers are especially critical of the company's policies regarding genetically modified seeds

   (B) the chemical and agricultural company Monsanto, with these writers being especially critical of the company's policies regarding genetically modified seeds

   (C) the chemical and agricultural company Monsanto; these writers have been especially critical of the company's policies regarding genetically modified seeds

   (D) the chemical and agricultural company Monsanto; these writers are especially critical and the company's policies regard genetically modified seeds

   (E) the chemical and agricultural company Monsanto; despite the company's policies regarding genetically modified seeds, these writers are especially critical

14. Although I agreed with the speaker's main points about the self-destructive pursuit of wealth, I could not bring myself to consent with her plan of offering less business and finance classes at the college level.

   (A) I could not bring myself to consent with her plan of offering less business and finance classes at the college level

   (B) I could not bring myself consenting to her plan to offer less business and finance classes at the college level

   (C) I could not bring myself to consent to her plan to have been offering less business and finance classes at the college level

   (D) I could not bring myself consenting to her plan of the offer, with fewer business and finance classes at the college level

   (E) I could not bring myself to consent to her plan to offer fewer business and finance classes at the college level

STOP

If you finish before time is called, you may check your work on this section only.
Do not turn to any other section in the test.

Chapter 18
PRACTICE TEST 4

Practice Test 4

SECTION 1
Time–25 minutes
35 Questions

1. Vampires, while predominantly recognized as part of European fantasy and mythology, is actually found in many Eastern cultures that have their own variations of these mythological creatures.

   (A) is actually found in many Eastern cultures that have their own variations
   (B) are actually found in many Eastern cultures that have their own variations
   (C) is actually found in many Eastern cultures that has its own variations
   (D) found in many Eastern cultures, are their own variations
   (E) Eastern cultures have their own variations of them and are found

2. In our own time, Steve Jobs and Elon Musk are two major examples of a businessman who have combined creative vision with technological expertise.

   (A) are two major examples of a businessman
   (B) are two major examples of businessmen
   (C) are a major example of businessmen
   (D) is a major example of two businessmen
   (E) is a major example of men being in business

3. The University of Santo Tomas in the Philippines stand as reminder of past Spanish imperialism and cultural inculcation through re-education practices.

   (A) stand as reminder of past Spanish imperialism
   (B) stands as reminders of past Spanish imperialism
   (C) stands as a reminder of past Spanish imperialism
   (D) stood as reminders by Spanish imperialism in the past
   (E) have stood as reminders about Spanish imperialism in the past

4. As a young adult in 1941, Jonathan Tillbury was a respectable fellow: he enjoyed genteel games like tennis, cricket, however playing polo rather than brutish sports.

   (A) he enjoyed genteel games like tennis, cricket, however playing polo
   (B) he enjoys genteel games like tennis, cricket, and polo
   (C) enjoying genteel games like tennis, cricket, and polo
   (D) he enjoyed genteel games like tennis, cricket, and polo
   (E) he played genteel games like tennis, cricket, and polo and he enjoyed them

5. Known as the quintessential love song, Roberta Flack, a legendary jazz and folk singer, popularized the tune "The First Time I Ever Saw Your Face" in 1972.

   (A) Roberta Flack, a legendary jazz and folk singer, popularized the tune "The First Time I Ever Saw Your Face"
   (B) "The First Time I Ever Saw Your Face", a jazz and folk singer, was as a song popularized by the legendary Roberta Flack
   (C) the legendary jazz and folk singer Robert Flack popularized "The First Time I Ever Saw Your Face"
   (D) "The First Time I Ever Saw Your Face", popularized by the legendary jazz and folk singer Roberta Flack was
   (E) "The First Time I Ever Saw Your Face" was popularized by the legendary jazz and folk singer Roberta Flack

6. The assigned gatherers in the tribe have been observed performing two actions: <u>collecting local herbs and plants, after given to the shaman for medicinal purposes.</u>

 (A) collecting local herbs and plants, after given to the shaman for medicinal purposes
 (B) having collected herbs and plants that were to be given to the shaman for medicinal purposes
 (C) collected local herbs and plants and gives them to the shaman for medicinal purposes
 (D) collect local herbs and plants and give them to the shaman for medicinal purposes
 (E) collecting local herbs and plants, and giving them to the shaman for medicinal purposes

7. <u>The archaeologist digging as the map had indicated, and he</u> was unable to recover the hidden artifacts that could have decrypted the ancient culture's language.

 (A) The archaeologist digging as the map had indicated, and he
 (B) The archaeologist digging as the map indicated but he
 (C) Although the archaeologist dug as the map indicates, he
 (D) Although the archaeologist dug as the map indicated, he
 (E) The archaeologist dug as the map has indicated, he however

8. Even though his parents had cautioned him against wandering into the forest, <u>Jeremy went exploring among the vines and leaves, who returned home with a terrible rash from poison ivy, validating his parents' worries.</u>

 (A) Jeremy went exploring among the vines and leaves, who returned home with a terrible rash from poison ivy, validating his parents' worries
 (B) Jeremy went exploring among the vines and leaves, he validated his parents' worries when he returned home with a terrible rash from poison ivy
 (C) Jeremy went exploring among the vines and leaves; validating his parents' worries, he returned home with a terrible rash from poison ivy
 (D) Jeremy, exploring among the vines and leaves, validated his parents' worries when he returns home with a terrible rash from poison ivy
 (E) Jeremy has explored among the vines and leaves, but he had returned home with a terrible rash from poison ivy, validating his parents' worries

9. <u>Because lacking motivation often leads to writing scenes that do not follow the story arc is the reason why screenwriters</u> are advised to take a day or two away from a script before revisions.

 (A) Because lacking motivation often leads to writing scenes that do not follow the story arc is the reason why screenwriters
 (B) Lacking motivation often leads to writing scenes that do not follow the story arc, and yet screenwriters
 (C) Because lacking motivation often leads to writing scenes that do not follow the story arc, screenwriters
 (D) The reason writing scenes that do not follow the story arc is from lacking motivation, which is why screenwriters
 (E) When the scene lacks motivation, the screenwriter does not follow the story arc, and because of this screenwriters

10. Graphic design, though among today's popular and increasingly high-paying careers, <u>is very difficult to explain to non-experts, which is often confusion with careers such as drawing and journalism.</u>

 (A) is very difficult to explain to non-experts, which is often confusion with careers such as drawing and journalism
 (B) is very difficult to explain to non-experts, who often confuse it with careers such as drawing and journalism
 (C) are very difficult, because to explain it to non-experts is to be confused with careers such as drawing and journalism
 (D) is very difficult to explain to non-experts, who often confuse it with careers, drawing, and journalism
 (E) are very difficult to explain to non-experts, where confusion is with careers such as drawing and journalism

11. Several prominent literary critics agree that *Bleak House* by Charles Dickens contains richer characters and more complicated social themes <u>than any novel</u> Dickens wrote.

 (A) than any novel
 (B) than any novel in addition that
 (C) of any novel
 (D) than any other novel
 (E) of any novel beyond this that

12. <u>Swimming until</u> two hours, Janet at last decided
     A

<u>to leave</u> the pool, fearing <u>that her</u> hands would
  B   C

prune forever were she to remain <u>in the water</u>
                                     D

much longer. <u>No error</u>
             E

13. John Lennon, a member of the Beatles,

<u>composing the song</u> "Imagine", which is
     A

<u>thought</u> by many <u>to be</u> an anthem <u>of</u> the social
  B   C   D

reform movements of the late 1970s. <u>No error</u>
                                E

14. <u>While many people</u> have great respect for the later,
     A

highly experimental <u>novels of</u> John Barth, I prefer
                  B

Barth's early works, which <u>to depict</u> life in
                     C

eastern Maryland with <u>intelligence and affection</u>.
                        D

<u>No error</u>
   E

15. <u>Despite</u> the growing popularity <u>of cuisine</u> from
     A   B

South America, many Peruvian restaurants

<u>has gone</u> out of business <u>in</u> the past five years.
 C   D

<u>No error</u>
   E

16. Susan <u>has began</u> writing a new series of books,
        A

each <u>of which</u> responds <u>to a work</u> of literature
    B   C

originally <u>published</u> in the nineteenth century.
          D

<u>No error</u>
   E

17. Louis <u>emerged from</u> his reality TV show as a crazy
        A

figure <u>whose</u> devilish antics are as likely to lead
        B

his family and friends into disaster <u>than to</u> propel
                          C

<u>his loved ones</u> to new heights of understanding.
   D

<u>No error</u>
   E

18. Doctor Richards <u>has successfully developed</u> a
               A

system for resolving workplace conflicts; if

widely adopted, <u>they could</u> make modern offices
             B

<u>much more pleasing</u> and hospitable <u>environments</u>.
     C   D

<u>No error</u>
   E

19. Before summer, <u>there is</u> usually <u>more than</u> ten
            A   B

women waiting in line to use <u>any one of</u> the
                      C

treadmills or stair machines at the small gym

<u>I normally visit</u>. <u>No error</u>
     D   E

20. It was very difficult for the different sections of the

jazz band <u>to harmonize</u> with one another, <u>since</u> the
        A   B

brass musicians <u>had not</u> had sufficient practice
           C

alongside <u>neither</u> the strings section or the
             D

woodwind section. <u>No error</u>
          E

Practice Test 4

21. Neither Gregory <u>or</u> Martha <u>believes</u> that a larger
                A   B

car, with <u>its</u> higher maintenance costs and greater
        C

gas consumption, <u>would be</u> a wise investment at
                  D

the present time. <u>No error</u>
                E

22. Over the past few years, <u>university courses</u> in
                            A

world literature have become <u>most inclusive</u> than
                           B

they once were; today, authors from Spain, South

Africa, and Indonesia <u>are</u> regularly included on
                      C

<u>a single syllabus</u>. <u>No error</u>
        D   E

23. A disturbing new collection of statistics <u>show that</u>
                                 A

young people <u>who work</u> in business and finance
              B

<u>are putting</u> in eighty-hour work weeks, often to the
      C

detriment of their <u>psychological and emotional</u>
                           D

well-being. <u>No error</u>
        E

24. If you compare <u>clothing</u> from the 1970s with
              A

clothing advertisements <u>from the present day,</u>
                   B

<u>you will</u> notice that today's ads depart from the
    C

earlier emphasis on sheer quantity and

<u>often feature</u> only a few well-selected items.
        D

<u>No error</u>
  E

25. While it may be possible for <u>the majority of</u> people
                         A

to learn from mistakes, <u>it is</u> equally true that some
                B

individuals <u>will always be</u> unresponsive <u>for even</u>
            C   D

the best constructive criticism. <u>No error</u>
                     E

26. <u>Some of</u> the ideas that <u>were recorded</u> in medieval
    A   B

scrolls remain <u>ambivalent</u> to this day; scholars
              C

continue to argue over the word <u>choices that</u> the
                      D

scrolls' authors use to express their points. <u>No error</u>
                        E

27. <u>Sumi was</u> not persuaded <u>to the arguments</u> of her
    A   B

colleagues and teachers, <u>who had</u> patiently
                C

explained that a few days of vacation would help

her <u>to combat exhaustion</u>. <u>No error</u>
       D   E

28. Students in fashion design courses <u>are taught</u> to use
                      A

colors that <u>compliment</u> each other; <u>for example,</u>
        B   C

cold blue tones should be posed against soft

<u>brown and orange hues</u>. <u>No error</u>
     D   E

29. Many of the scenes of dialogue <u>in the movie</u> were
                     A

filmed <u>on location</u> in Finland, <u>as well as</u> the most
      B   C

important battle sequences <u>were filmed</u> at a
                D

soundstage in California. <u>No error</u>
                E

18   **18**   **18**   **18**   **18**   **18**   **18**

Unauthorized copying or
reuse of any part of this
page is illegal.

(1) In movies, television shows, and political cartoons, we are often faced with a common depiction: stern and authoritative parents, opposed by spontaneous and rebellious teenagers. (2) Who doesn't remember films like *Fast Times at Ridgemont High* or *Orange County*, where young adults seem to be breaking all their parents' rules? (3) As much as we enjoy entertainment like this, the real situation today is turning into something quite different. (4) Teenagers no longer see parents as the enemy; instead, parents and teens to strike up relationships built on trust, cooperation, and mutual respect.

(5) This shift in attitudes has been recognized by specialists in sociology and psychology. (6) "In a competitive job market and a world transformed by technology, teens realize that opposing their parents can be self-destructive," says Thomas Jarrell, a professor at the University of Colorado. (7) Based on this specific example, it can be seen that parents are valued as guides to an uncertain and rapidly-changing adolescent world. (8) In one of his articles, Jarrell describes a young man in an AP Economics class; in order to succeed in his studies, this student regularly asks his father, an employee at the World Bank, about the most important issues in finance. (9) Any other example of this sort of productive parent-child relationship can be found in almost every high school in America, a far cry from the teenage rebellion of decades ago.

30. Which of the following, if inserted before sentence 1, would make the most effective introduction to the essay?

(A) Audiences in the 1980s were among the first to see the parents-versus-teenagers romantic comedy come into its own as a popular form of cinema.
(B) One of the greatest dangers that teenagers today face is not a physical adversary; rather, it is the "enemy" represented by conformity and peer pressure.
(C) The relationship between parents and children has often been understood as a conflict of irreconcilable wills and desires.
(D) Students today face an employment environment where, even upon successful graduation from college, job opportunities can remain uncertain.
(E) A new set of interactions between parents and children has been explained by groundbreaking research originating in universities on the American West Coast.

31. What is the best substitute for the phrase "like this" in sentence 3?

(A) that portrays amicable relationships
(B) that highlights contentious behavior
(C) which Hollywood lionizes
(D) which few people truly understand
(E) that teenagers seldom respect

32. Which of the following is the best version of the underlined portion of sentence 4 (reproduced below)?

Teenagers no longer see parents as the enemy; instead, parents and teens to strike up relationships built on trust, cooperation, and mutual respect.

(A) (as it is now)
(B) parents and teens instead striking up relationships, they are
(C) parents are striking up relationships and also teens
(D) parents and teens are striking up relationships
(E) where parents and teens strike up relationships

33. What is the best location for sentence 7?

(A) (Where it is now)
(B) After sentence 2
(C) After sentence 3
(D) After sentence 8
(E) After sentence 9

34. Which of the following is the best version of the underlined portion of sentence 9 (reproduced below)?

Any other example of this sort of productive parent-child relationship can be found in almost every high school in America, a far cry from the teenage rebellion of decades ago.

(A) (As it is now)
(B) Another example of this sort, being a productive parent-child relationship
(C) Other examples of this sort are productive parent-child relationships and those
(D) Another example where the parent-child relationship is productive
(E) Other examples of productive parent-child relationships

35. Which of the following would make the most logical final sentence for the essay?

(A) It is possible that the entertainment of years ago, such as single-player arcade games, simply encouraged adolescents to retreat into themselves and shun the aid of their families.
(B) This generation gap is also being eradicated by a new set of network sitcoms, which emphasize comfortable family relationships over the allure of teenage rebellion.
(C) Nonetheless, it seems unlikely that Jarrell's findings can explain how younger children, such as toddlers, learn to interact within modern families.
(D) Success for young people, today, is premised on working within family structures that create cooperation and understanding.
(E) Jarrell has also observed college students who are on track to become doctors or engineers and who find their families' high expectations invigorating rather than confining.

STOP
If you finish before time is called, you may check your work on this section only.
Do not turn to any other section in the test.

SECTION 2
Time–10 minutes
14 Questions

1. There is a problem with <u>your recent biomedical research proposal, it completely neglects</u> the recent research that has been performed on the genetic roots of chronic diseases.

(A) your recent biomedical research proposal, it completely neglects
(B) your recent biomedical research proposal, completely neglects
(C) your recent biomedical research proposal although it completely neglects
(D) your recent biomedical research proposal where it is completely neglecting
(E) your recent biomedical research proposal, which completely neglects

2. An avid collector of sporting memorabilia, Mr. Margrave was truly dispirited to find that the selection of cards at the Boston Historical Society <u>did not even rival his hometown museum.</u>

(A) did not even rival his hometown museum
(B) did not even rival the selection at his hometown museum
(C) not even rivaling his hometown museum and its selection
(D) not even rivaling the museum in his hometown
(E) did not even have his hometown museum as their rival for selection

3. I really enjoy going to movies that have romantic twists as part of the plot line, particularly <u>when such twists lead to marriage and celebration.</u>

(A) when such twists lead to marriage and celebration
(B) the twist leading to marriage, also celebration
(C) such a twist has led to marriage and celebration
(D) the twist is one that is leading to marriage and celebration
(E) the twist will have led from marriage and celebration

4. Duncan Sheik, a popular musician from the 1990s, wrote the music and lyrics to *Spring Awakening*, a rock musical adaptation <u>of the modernist play for the same name</u>.

(A) of the modernist play for the same name
(B) about the modernist play with the same name
(C) of the modernist play of the same name
(D) in the modernist play of the same name
(E) on modernity with a play of the same name

5. Contrary to popular belief, Asian Americans vastly impacted the civil rights movement of the 1960s; <u>but one such minority leader was Yuri Kochiyama, a Japanese-American human rights activist</u> who regularly consulted Malcom X.

(A) but one such minority leader was Yuri Kochiyama, a Japanese-American human rights activist
(B) one such minority leader was Yuri Kochiyama, a Japanese-American human rights activist
(C) and Yuri Kochiyama, a Japanese-American human rights activist, is one such minority leader
(D) and a Japanese-American human rights activist, Yuri Kochiyama, was one such minority leader
(E) a Japanese-American rights activist, Yuri Kochiyama, led minorities

6. The primary cathedral of the city of Florence, <u>the Basilica of Saint Mary of the Flower is famous for its massive sectioned dome and its stonework which is contrasted</u>.

(A) the Basilica of Saint Mary of the Flower is famous for its massive sectioned dome and its stonework which is contrasted
(B) the massive sectioned dome and the contrasted stonework are what make the Basilica of Saint Mary of the Flower famous
(C) what makes the Basilica of Saint Mary of the Flower famous are its massive sectioned dome and its contrasting stonework
(D) the Basilica of Saint Mary of the Flower, is famous for its massive sectioned dome and its contrasting stonework
(E) the Basilica of Saint Mary of the flower is famous, its dome is massive and its contrasting stonework

7. A critic of e-mail and other messaging systems, author Sherry Turkle has written a new book deriding <u>the forms of technology and they are, according to her, destroying our ability to communicate.</u>

   (A) the forms of technology and they are, according to her, destroying our ability to communicate
   (B) the forms of technology that, according to her, are destroying our ability to communicate
   (C) how, according to her, forms of technology are destroying our ability to communicate
   (D) forms of technology, when according to her they are destroying our ability to communicate
   (E) technology that, according to her, destroys our ability to communicate in its forms

8. After finding that the enrollment of the course she wanted to take, a seminar on child psychology, <u>had already been filled, Marcy instead signing up for a lecture course on the history of children's literature.</u>

   (A) had already been filled, Marcy instead signing up for a lecture course on the history of children's literature
   (B) had been filled, Marcy instead was to sign up for a lecture course which is the history of children's literature
   (C) already being filled, Marcy instead signed up for a lecture course, it was history of children's literature
   (D) had already been filled, a lecture course on the history of children's literature was what Marcy signed up for instead
   (E) had already been filled, Marcy signed up for a lecture course on the history of children's literature instead

9. German poet Rainer Maria Rilke is well known for his compositions in verse, <u>yet is perhaps more famous from the writer of his autobiographical novel *The Notebooks of Malte Laurids Brigge*.</u>

   (A) yet is perhaps more famous from the writer of his autobiographical novel *The Notebooks of Malte Laurids Brigge*
   (B) perhaps more famously he is the writer of the autobiographical novel *The Notebooks of Malte Laurids Brigge*
   (C) in addition he is more famous as the writer of his autobiographical novel *The Notebooks of Malte Laurids Brigge*
   (D) since he is more famous for being the writer of the autobiographical novel *The Notebooks of Malte Laurids Brigge*
   (E) yet is perhaps more famous for his autobiographical novel *The Notebooks of Malte Laurids Brigge*

10. After learning that profits had fallen drastically, <u>shares of David's business were rapidly sold off by his investors, leaving his finances and future prospects in a precarious state.</u>

   (A) shares of David's business were rapidly sold off by his investors, leaving his finances and future prospects in a precarious state
   (B) investors rapidly sold off shares of David's business, leaving his finances and future prospects in a precarious state
   (C) David and his business were rapidly sold off by his investors, his finances and future leaving the prospects in a precarious state
   (D) shares of David's business being rapidly sold off, his investors leaving his finances and future prospects in a precarious state
   (E) investors rapidly sold their shares of David's business; consequently, his finances and future prospects left in a precarious state

11. By buying a few basic materials from your local hardware store and following a simple instruction manual, <u>a pinewood derby car is easy to construct so that you meet</u> standard length and weight requirements.

   (A) a pinewood derby car is easy to construct so that you meet
   (B) a pinewood derby car can be constructed, and you can meet
   (C) you can easily construct a pinewood derby car that meets
   (D) you can construct a pinewood derby car, and it meets
   (E) your construction of a pinewood derby car will meet

145

Practice Test 4

12. The patients in the physiological experiment have asserted that, as the result of stimulation by an electric apparatus, <u>they can see jewel-like colors and can hear sounds that recall horns and tubas.</u>

    (A) they can see jewel-like colors and can hear sounds that recall horns and tubas
    (B) they can see and hear jewel-like colors and sounds that recall horns and tubas
    (C) they can see jewel-like colors and sounds that recall horns and tubas can be heard
    (D) they can see jewel-like colors, in addition hearing sounds that recall horns and tubas
    (E) they can see jewel-like colors, although sounds that recall horns and tubas are heard as well

13. The easiest way to destroy a tall tree is <u>cutting a ring in the trunk just a few feet from the ground, then to fell</u> the tree as soon as the sap has dried and the wood has weakened.

    (A) cutting a ring in the trunk just a few feet from the ground, then to fell
    (B) to cut a ring in the trunk just a few feet from the ground, then to fell
    (C) cutting a ring in the trunk just a few feet from the ground and also felling
    (D) when you cut a ring in the trunk just a few feet from the ground, then felling
    (E) to cut a ring in the trunk just a few feet from the ground after you fell

14. In a tract of his known as *The Phaedrus*, <u>one of the world's best-known arguments in favor of organizing society around non-written communication is presented by the philosopher Plato.</u>

    (A) one of the world's best-known arguments in favor of organizing society around non-written communication is presented by the philosopher Plato
    (B) in favor of organizing society around non-written communication, one of the world's best-known arguments had been presented by Plato, who was a philosopher
    (C) the philosopher Plato presents one of the world's best-known arguments in favor of organizing society around non-written communication
    (D) organizing society around non-written communication is one of the best-known arguments favored and presented by the philosopher Plato
    (E) the philosopher Plato, who will have favored organizing society around non-written communication, presents one of the world's best-known arguments

STOP
If you finish before time is called, you may check your work on this section only.
Do not turn to any other section in the test.

Chapter 19
PRACTICE TEST 5

SECTION 1
Time–25 minutes
35 Questions

1. Easter Island, which is famous for its mysterious stone sculptures, <u>nonetheless seldom visited</u> by tourists.

   (A) nonetheless seldom visited
   (B) is nonetheless seldom visited
   (C) visited seldom in contrast to this
   (D) is nonetheless seldom to be visited
   (E) nonetheless will be seldom visited

2. Legendary pianist Glenn Gould <u>spent the last years of his life and avoided</u> live performance of any sort, composing innovative multi-track recordings instead.

   (A) spent the last years of his life and avoided
   (B) spent the last years of his life avoiding
   (C) he spent the last years of his life, then avoided
   (D) spent the last years of his life, and to avoid
   (E) spending his life, the last years of it avoiding

3. <u>Although the European car market is now dominated by Italy, Britain, and especially cars originating from Germany</u>, France once possessed a robust automotive industry.

   (A) Although the European car market is now dominated by Italy, Britain, and especially cars originating from Germany
   (B) In spite of the European car market now being dominated by Italy, Britain, and especially cars originating from Germany
   (C) Although the European car market is now dominated by Italy, Britain, and especially Germany
   (D) The European car market is now dominated by Italy, Britain, and especially Germany
   (E) Although Italy, Britain, and especially Germany now dominates the European car market

4. <u>Contrasting against</u> many of the other innovative painters of his time, Paul Gauguin received little formal academic training.

   (A) Contrasting against
   (B) Contrary against
   (C) In contrast against
   (D) Unlike to
   (E) In contrast to

5. The <u>healthier and lighter snack was made available</u> on the school lunch menu to combat growing childhood obesity.

   (A) healthier and lighter snack was made available
   (B) healthy and lighter snack had been made available
   (C) healthy and light snack were now available
   (D) snack, healthier and light, were made available
   (E) snacks, healthy and lighter, were made available

6. A study sponsored by the University of Southern California has shown that, <u>if one does not stand up and stretch at least once every two hours</u>, your posture and stamina will suffer.

   (A) if one does not stand up and stretch at least once every two hours
   (B) if one is not standing up and stretching at least once every two hours
   (C) if one either does not stand up nor stretches at least once every two hours
   (D) if you do not stand up and stretch at least once every two hours
   (E) if you do not stand up and stretch instead at least once every two hours

7. <u>Famous both for its insatiable appetite as well as having eyesight which is poor</u>, the tapir is a large mammal that can be found in the grasslands of central Africa.

(A) Famous both for its insatiable appetite as well as having eyesight which is poor
(B) Famous for eating insatiably and it has poor eyesight in addition to this
(C) Famous both for its insatiable appetite and for its poor eyesight
(D) Famous from having insatiability in its eating and in its poor eyesight
(E) Because its appetite is famously insatiable and its eyesight is extremely poor

8. Mesmerized by the shimmering golden color, which is reminiscent of golden sunlight, <u>blonde hair fascinates many people</u>.

(A) blonde hair fascinates many people
(B) fascinating to many people is blonde hair
(C) many people are fascinated by blonde hair
(D) blond hair is one of the fascinations of many people
(E) many people have been found with fascination from blonde hair

9. Despite experiencing impoverished living conditions and possible bouts of insanity, <u>"The Tell-Tale Heart" and "The Raven" earned the writer Edgar Allan Poe respect after his death</u>.

(A) "The Tell-Tale Heart" and "The Raven" earned the writer Edgar Allan Poe respect after his death
(B) Edgar Allan Poe earned respect after his death for writings such as "The Raven" and "The Tell-Tale Heart"
(C) "The Tell-Tale Heart" and "The Raven" were written to earn Edgar Allan Poe respect after he died
(D) respect came after death to Edgar Allan Poe, who wrote "The Tell-Tale Heart" and "The Raven"
(E) Edgar Allan Poe before his death wrote "The Tell-Tale Heart" and "The Raven" with respect earned for his writings

10. <u>James was enormously unhappy with his family Christmas photo, because he vowed to hire a more accomplished photographer and obtained better lighting for next year's photo shoot.</u>

(A) James was enormously unhappy with his family Christmas photo, because he vowed to hire a more accomplished photographer and obtained better lighting for next year's photo shoot.
(B) Enormously unhappy with his family Christmas photo, James vowed to hire a more accomplished photographer and obtain better lighting for next year's photo shoot.
(C) James, being enormously unhappy with his family Christmas photo, when he vowed to hire a more accomplished photographer and obtain better lighting for next year's photo shoot.
(D) His family Christmas photo making him enormously unhappy, James's vow was to hire a more accomplished photographer and obtain better lighting for next year's photo shoot.
(E) With hiring a more accomplished photographer and obtaining better lighting for next year's photo shoot, James vows he will have been enormously unhappy with his family Christmas photo.

11. When I was young, <u>my family enjoyed visiting Montreal, this partially explaining why I later enrolled at one of the most dynamic colleges in the city, McGill University</u>.

(A) my family enjoyed visiting Montreal, this partially explaining why I later enrolled at one of the most dynamic colleges in the city, McGill University
(B) my family enjoyed visiting Montreal, it partially explains why I later enrolled at one of the most dynamic colleges in the city, McGill University
(C) my family and I enjoyed visiting Montreal; this partially explains why I later enrolled at one of the most dynamic colleges in the city, McGill University
(D) my family enjoyed visiting Montreal; explaining partially why I later enrolled at one of the most dynamic colleges in the city, which is McGill University
(E) Montreal was a place my family enjoyed visiting; from this situation, it partially explains why I later enrolled at one of the most dynamic colleges in the city, McGill University

19   19   19   19   19   19   19

Unauthorized copying or reuse of any part of this page is illegal.

12. When asked by the visiting speaker what their
    A   B
career goals were, many of the high school

students declared that they wanted to be lawyers
            C
or a doctor later in life. No error
    D   E

13. A student of the art of pottery must not only
                    A
develop their ability to coordinate form and color,
    B   C
but also acquire at least a rudimentary awareness of

industrial methods and modern material science.
        D
No error
    E

14. The pristine architecture of Inigo Jones was part of
                                              A
the sixteenth and seventeenth-century classical

revival, it swept through both Jones's England and
         B   C
many of the countries of Continental Europe.
              D
No error
    E

15. The large gray umbrella that Philip had brought
                            A
with him turned out to be uselessly on account of
          B   C
the clear skies and beautiful weather. No error
                  D   E

16. It soon became clear not only that Kevin was
              A   B
completely unprepared for his class presentation,

and also that his research figures were plagiarized
    C
from unreliable sources. No error
        D   E

17. A festival for both emerging and established
                    A
voices in international art, the Whitney Biennale
    B
attracts sculptors, painters, and video art from
    C   D
every continent on the globe. No error
                                E

18. I have long been concerned in raising funds
                    A
to benefit the homeless in my area, but I am
    B   C
worried that my funds will make their way to
                        D
corrupt or dishonest nonprofit organizations.

No error
    E

19. It is considered old-fashioned by many, the musical
    A   B
Guys and Dolls still delivers a message of
                C
responsibility and maturity that is highly relevant
                            D
to our own time. No error
                    E

20. The poem "Theme for English B" by Langston

Hughes describes a young man who must deal with
        A   B
a routine and potentially dull writing assignment;
        C
ironically, the poem is now teaching to English
                            D
students as an example of the power of

self-expression. No error
                    E

21. Without either the <u>votes needed</u> to defeat his
                       A

    opponent in the primaries <u>nor sufficient</u> funds to
                             B

    run as an independent candidate, Senator Kroll

    <u>decided</u> to leave Washington <u>and begin</u> a new
      C   D

    career as an independent businessman. <u>No error</u>
                                   E

22. The tennis coach <u>told</u> Shawn <u>and me</u> that we need
                 A   B

    to buy <u>headbands</u> and wristbands in the team color
            C

    <u>and wearing</u> them to the next practice. <u>No error</u>
      D   E

23. <u>According to</u> recent statistics, young Americans
     A

    <u>are hesitant to</u> buy new houses and are
       B

    <u>increasing likely</u> <u>to take out</u> long-term leases
       C   D

    on apartments. <u>No error</u>
               E

24. Flapping its wings furiously, the bat <u>swooping</u> low
                            A

    just <u>over our heads,</u> <u>then</u> made a sudden turn
           B   C

    upward and <u>disappeared</u> into the dark blue evening
             D

    sky. <u>No error</u>
         E

25. For decades, the California Condor <u>was thought</u> to
                           A

    be <u>on the verge</u> of extinction, but in the 1980s this
      B

    species of large vulture <u>will begin</u> <u>to thrive</u> once
                  C   D

    again on the American West Coast. <u>No error</u>
                          E

26. Mrs. Holloway may teach <u>less than</u> fifteen
                    A

    students in some of her classes, <u>but</u> this does
                         B

    not mean <u>that she</u> is an unpopular instructor;
           C

    <u>her</u> seminars are simply scheduled at rather
     D

    inconvenient times. <u>No error</u>
                E

27. The search <u>committee respected</u> Ronald not so
           A

    much for his fifteen years of on-the-job experience

    <u>but because of</u> his ability <u>to remain</u> calm
           B   C

    <u>and collected</u> in extremely tense situations.
       D

    <u>No error</u>
      E

28. By the time we <u>arrived</u> at the shopping mall and
               A

    made our way to the sale, the store <u>sold all</u> the
                         B

    <u>parkas and moccasins</u> that had been <u>on discount.</u>
          C   D

    <u>No error</u>
      E

29. In the small French town <u>of Saint Malo,</u>
                   A

    <u>which is located</u> in sight of the English Channel,
          B

    <u>an annual</u> celebration <u>of culture and history</u> from
      C   D

    the Middle Ages is held every year. <u>No error</u>
                          E

Practice Test 5

19 19 19 19 19 19 19

Unauthorized copying or reuse of any part of this page is illegal.

(1) An estuary has a unique duality in its nature. (2) It is an area where a body of fresh water, such as a flowing river, meets the salt water in an ocean. (3) One can think of an estuary as a transitional area, where forms of life from two very different ecosystems meet. (4) Here, you will find sandy river deltas, teeming marshes and swamps, and other low-lying zones where unique forms of life reside. (5) Looking at an estuary, it is possible to feel transported back to an earlier stage of the history of animal life, when primitive fish and eels first spawned legs and began to move onto dry land.

(6) The animals in today's estuaries, though, are no less exciting. (7) Visitors to the estuaries of Florida will see majestic nautical birds such as pink flamingos, white egrets, and will discover brilliant scarlet ibises as well. (8) A few lucky people might also get a glimpse of a manatee, a good-natured nautical mammal that looks a little like walruses do.

(9) Often, pollutants from factories are washed downriver, passing through sensitive estuary regions before spreading out into the sea. (10) It is crucial for us to protect these special habitats, not only because of their splendid wildlife, but also because they provide so many people with fresh fish and other indispensable natural resources.

30. Which of the following revisions is most needed in sentence 3 (reproduced below)?

One can think of an estuary as a transitional area, where forms of life from two very different ecosystems meet.

(A) Change "one" to "you".
(B) Change "can think" to "could have thought".
(C) Change "where" to "in which".
(D) Change the comma to a semicolon.
(E) Insert "and" after the comma.

31. In context, what is the best revision of sentence 5 (reproduced below)?

Looking at an estuary, it is possible to feel transported back to an earlier stage of the history of animal life, when primitive fish and eels first spawned legs and began to move onto dry land.

(A) While looking at an estuary, it is possible to feel transported back to an earlier stage in the history of animal life, a time when primitive fish and eels first spawned legs, moving onto dry land.
(B) When looking at an estuary, a place where primitive fish and eels first spawned legs and began to move onto dry land, it is possible to feel transported back to animal life's earlier stage in history.
(C) You can look at an estuary, and possibly you will feel transported back to an earlier stage of the history of animal life where primitive fish and eels first spawned legs and began to move onto dry land.
(D) Primitive fish and eels first spawned legs and began to move onto dry land in estuaries, when you can feel transported back to an earlier stage of the history of animal life.
(E) Looking at an estuary, you can feel transported back to an earlier stage of the history of animal life, when primitive fish and eels first spawned legs and began to move onto dry land.

32. In context, the underlined portion of sentence 7 (reproduced below) could best be revised in which of the following ways?

Visitors to the estuaries of Florida will see majestic nautical birds such as <u>*pink flamingos, white egrets, and will discover brilliant scarlet ibises as well*</u>

(A) (as it is now)
(B) pink flamingos, white egrets, and scarlet ibises which are brilliant
(C) pink flamingos, white egrets, in addition they will discover brilliant scarlet ibises
(D) the pink flamingo, white egret, or brilliant scarlet ibis
(E) pink flamingos, white egrets, and brilliant scarlet ibises

33. Which of the following is the best version of the underlined portion of sentence 8 (reproduced below)?

A few lucky people might also get a glimpse of a manatee, a good-natured nautical mammal <u>*that looks a little like walruses do.*</u>

(A) (as it is now)
(B) which looks a little like walruses
(C) that looks a little like a walrus
(D) that, like a walrus, shares a similar look
(E) in which they look a little like walruses

34. Which of the following sentences, if inserted before sentence 9, would most improve the third paragraph?

(A) There are many other organisms that face the likelihood of becoming endangered if we do not continue to employ wise conservation practices.
(B) Yet bird populations worldwide continue to dwindle because of human encroachment.
(C) There is hope that the animals that inhabit estuaries can be saved through the adoption of alternative fishing and foresting methods.
(D) Unfortunately, many of the most beautiful estuaries are under attack from commercial development.
(E) Without the manatee, the delicate ecological balance found in Florida estuaries would be disrupted and serious ramifications for many estuary food chains would follow.

35. Which of the following, if placed after sentence 10, would be the most effective concluding sentence for the essay?

(A) A well-protected estuary is not simply an example of brilliant animal diversity: it is also an example of humanity's stewardship of nature, and a boon to society for generations.
(B) Many people neither understand nor value the benefits to be gained from preserving these estuaries, and such negligence will lead to the mass extinction of endangered animals.
(C) Pollutants that corrupt the river can be replaced by alternative industrial materials that can be captured and disposed of in secure locations with much greater ease.
(D) Should our protection of such special habitats cease, familiar estuary species will be forced to adapt in new ways in order to ensure their long-term survival.
(E) The salt content from the aggregation of fresh and ocean water provides perfect conditions for organisms that might not be able to survive for long in more humid freshwater swamps.

STOP

**If you finish before time is called, you may check your work on this section only.
Do not turn to any other section in the test.**

SECTION 2
Time–10 minutes
14 Questions

1. Following much consideration of all the boarding school options available, Sinéad <u>eventually deciding</u> to send her daughter to a small private academy in rural Maine.

   (A) eventually deciding
   (B) decided it eventually
   (C) eventually in decision to
   (D) eventually was decided
   (E) eventually decided

2. The Spartans were able to build a successful Greek city-state on account of <u>their efficient civic planning, their disciplined military training, and they were devoted to common values</u>.

   (A) their efficient civic planning, their disciplined military training, and they were devoted to common values
   (B) their efficient civic planning, their disciplined military training, and their devotion to common values
   (C) them being devoted to efficient civic planning, disciplined military training, as well as common values
   (D) their efficient civic planning, they had also disciplined military training and were devoted to common values
   (E) when they had efficient civic planning, their disciplined military training, and their devotion to common values

3. Both Tom Wolfe and Hunter S. Thompson helped to re-define the role of journalism <u>in the 1960s, Wolfe alone went on to make significant contributions to the art of the novel</u>.

   (A) in the 1960s, Wolfe alone went on to make significant contributions to the art of the novel
   (B) in the 1960s; Wolfe alone making significant contributions to the art of the novel
   (C) in the 1960s; therefore, Wolfe alone went on to make significant contributions to the art of the novel
   (D) in the 1960s, and indeed Wolfe alone went on to make significant contributions to the art of the novel
   (E) in the 1960s, but Wolfe alone went on to make significant contributions to the art of the novel

4. The fantasy novel series *Song of Ice and Fire* by George R.R. Martin is currently <u>a bestseller, it also serves</u> as the basis of the popular television show *Game of Thrones*.

   (A) a bestseller, it also serves
   (B) a bestseller, also serving in addition
   (C) a bestseller; in addition, this series serves
   (D) a bestseller, which also had been serving
   (E) a bestseller; serving also

5. After performing as a dancer with the New York City Ballet for almost a decade, Kyle <u>would be beginning</u> a new career as a ballet photographer.

   (A) would be beginning
   (B) began
   (C) beginning
   (D) is to have begun
   (E) would make a beginning of

6. <u>Among the most important novelists in early twentieth-century Japan was Yasunari Kawabata and Junichiro Tanizaki</u>, both of whom documented the struggles faced by their country's rising middle class.

   (A) Among the most important novelists in early twentieth-century Japan was Yasunari Kawabata and Junichiro Tanizaki
   (B) Among the important novelist group in early twentieth-century Japan was Yasunari Kawabata and Junichiro Tanizaki
   (C) Among the most important novelists in early twentieth-century Japan was either Yasunari Kawabata or Junichiro Tanizaki
   (D) Among the most important novelists in early twentieth-century Japan were Yasunari Kawabata and Junichiro Tanizaki
   (E) Among the most important novelists in early twentieth-century Japan will have been Yasunari Kawabata and Junichiro Tanizaki

7. Nutritionists have argued that strawberries contain more essential nutrients <u>than eating either blueberries or blackberries</u>.

   (A) than eating either blueberries or blackberries
   (B) either than eating blueberries or blackberries
   (C) than either blueberries and also blackberries
   (D) than either blueberries or blackberries do
   (E) than blueberries nor blackberries do when eaten

8. Although John initially performed aerobics with dead weights in order to strengthen his core muscle groups, <u>a more efficient technique was developed from him later in his bodybuilding career.</u>

   (A) a more efficient technique was developed from him later in his bodybuilding career
   (B) he developed a more efficient technique later in his bodybuilding career
   (C) he was later to have developing a more efficient technique in his bodybuilding career
   (D) he later will develop a technique that had been more efficient for his bodybuilding career
   (E) his bodybuilding career was later to develop a more efficient technique

9. <u>From keeping accurate records</u> of every butterfly he ever observed in the wild, Clark created a personal archive that even a professionally-trained entomologist would envy.

   (A) From keeping accurate records
   (B) Because he will keep accurate records
   (C) Because of keeping accurate records
   (D) Despite keeping accurate records
   (E) By keeping accurate records

10. A classic film by French director Jean-Pierre Melville, <u>the members of the French Resistance are depicted in an appreciative yet straightforward manner in *Army of Shadows*.</u>

   (A) the members of the French Resistance are depicted in an appreciative yet straightforward manner in *Army of Shadows*
   (B) an appreciative yet straightforward manner is used to depict the members of the French Resistance in *Army of Shadows*
   (C) *Army of Shadows* depicts the members of the French Resistance in an appreciative yet straightforward manner
   (D) *Army of Shadows* depicts the members of the French Resistance, in which it uses an appreciative yet straightforward manner
   (E) the depiction of the French Resistance in *Army of Shadows* is appreciative yet straightforward

11. <u>A semi-autonomous institution that had specialized in the art of the Middle Ages and the early Renaissance</u>, the Cloisters Museum is located only a convenient bus-ride away from its parent institution, the Museum of Modern Art.

   (A) A semi-autonomous institution that had specialized in the art of the Middle Ages and the early Renaissance
   (B) Specializing in the art of the Middle Ages and the early Renaissance, which makes it semi-autonomous for an institution
   (C) Specializing the art of the Middle Ages and the early Renaissance and being a semi-autonomous institution
   (D) Specializing in the art of the Middle Ages and the early Renaissance, where it is also a semi-autonomous institution
   (E) A semi-autonomous institution that specializes in the art of the Middle Ages and the early Renaissance

12. Though conventional wisdom says that you should eat less to lose weight, eating only one large meal a day actually does less for your health <u>as</u> eating four small meals a day.

   (A) as
   (B) than
   (C) in comparison with
   (D) in opposition to
   (E) than that of

Practice Test 5

13. Over the past decade, the journalistic profession has expanded radically; <u>by simply starting a blog or an online newsletter, the classification of "journalist" can be assumed</u>.

(A) by simply starting a blog or an online newsletter, the classification of "journalist" can be assumed

(B) one can start a blog or an online newsletter, where the classification of "journalist" can simply be assumed

(C) one can assume the classification of "journalist" simply by starting a blog or an online newsletter

(D) by simply starting a blog or an online newsletter, the classification of "journalist" is what one assumes

(E) one can assume the classification of "journalist" because one is simply starting a blog or an online newsletter

14. The policy recommendations of the mayor, who wants to revitalize the downtown area, <u>has been focused on increasing building height and creating tax incentives</u>.

(A) has been focused on increasing building height and creating tax incentives

(B) was being focused on increasing building height and creating tax incentives

(C) that are focused on increasing building height and creating tax incentives

(D) are focused with increased building heights and created tax incentives

(E) are focused on increasing building height and creating tax incentives

STOP
**If you finish before time is called, you may check your work on this section only.
Do not turn to any other section in the test.**

(ANSWERS ON PAGE 209)

Chapter 20
PRACTICE TEST 6

SECTION 1
Time–25 minutes
35 Questions

1. In an effort to bring high quality medical care to underprivileged populations, physician and anthropologist Paul Farmer <u>working with other humanitarians to found</u> the Partners in Health hospital in Haiti.

   (A) working with other humanitarians to found
   (B) work with other humanitarians to found
   (C) worked with other humanitarians to found
   (D) worked with other humanitarians, founded
   (E) to work with other humanitarians to found

2. Opened in 1949, the jazz club known as Birdland <u>soon became</u> a premier performance space for such musical legends as John Coltrane and Miles Davis.

   (A) soon became
   (B) soon becoming
   (C) would have become
   (D) that soon became
   (E) soon it became

3. The ancient Egyptians, who are best known for creating the pyramids at Giza, not only built monumental landmarks but also <u>early toothpaste and eye makeup were created by them</u>.

   (A) early toothpaste and eye makeup were created by them
   (B) they created early toothpaste and eye makeup
   (C) who created early toothpaste and eye makeup
   (D) creating early toothpaste and eye makeup
   (E) created early toothpaste and eye makeup

4. Prior to the economic collapse of 2008, many Americans bought homes at high prices and high interest <u>rates, due to this many struggling homeowners failed to pay their mortgages and subsequently lost their homes</u>.

   (A) rates, due to this many struggling homeowners failed to pay their mortgages and subsequently lost their homes
   (B) rates, this is the reason why many struggling homeowners failed to pay their mortgages and subsequently were losing their homes
   (C) rates; therefore, many struggling homeowners failed to pay their mortgages and subsequently lost their homes
   (D) rates, many struggling homeowners then failed to pay their mortgages and subsequently lost their homes
   (E) rates; because of that, many struggling homeowners failed to pay their mortgages and subsequently had lost their homes

5. Though several inventors in the nineteenth century endeavored to create a functional telegraph, Samuel Morse fought vigorously to have sole credit for the <u>idea, he received the patent in 1847</u>.

   (A) idea, he received the patent in 1847
   (B) idea, and he received the patent in 1847
   (C) idea; and he received the patent in 1847
   (D) idea, yet he received the patent in 1847
   (E) idea, to receive the patent in 1847

6. <u>He would not have spent</u> so much time vacationing in Cuba, Ernest Hemingway might never have become the island nation's most beloved American author.

   (A) He would not have spent
   (B) Without him spending
   (C) Were he not to spend
   (D) If he was not spending
   (E) Had he not spent

7. A legendary distance runner, Steve Prefontaine was stubborn about leading the pack for the duration of the race, rather than saving his energy for the end as a way <u>to prove to him</u> that he truly had more speed and endurance than his competitors.

   (A) to prove to him
   (B) of proving
   (C) for proving to himself
   (D) where he proved
   (E) in which he is proven

8. The health benefits of exercise may outweigh <u>a proper diet</u>, although both a healthy diet and an appropriate exercise routine are highly recommended for a fulfilling lifestyle.

   (A) a proper diet
   (B) each maintaining a proper diet
   (C) of a proper diet
   (D) those of a proper diet
   (E) that of a proper diet

9. In the United States during the 1950s, a booming population, as well as a high national morale, <u>that led to</u> a growing domestic economy spurred by home and car purchases.

   (A) that led to
   (B) leading to
   (C) will lead to
   (D) has led to
   (E) led to

10. His excellence in the art of translation and in the subtleties of verse form <u>has made</u> Charles Martin one of the most revered "poet's poets" currently writing.

   (A) has made
   (B) have made
   (C) had made
   (D) were making
   (E) are to make

11. The original rendition of the Mr. Peanut advertising mascot was drawn with a realistic monocle and a meticulously detailed peanut shell; <u>however, its gradual evolution from this early version into the simpler, streamlined cartoon image that is popular today.</u>

   (A) however, its gradual evolution from this early version into the simpler, streamlined cartoon image that is popular today
   (B) however, Mr. Peanut gradually evolved, although he is the simpler, streamlined cartoon image popular today
   (C) however, this early version gradually evolved into the simpler, streamlined cartoon image that is popular today
   (D) popular today, however, is the simpler, streamlined cartoon image of Mr. Peanut and his gradual evolution
   (E) however, this popular version will gradually evolve into what is today a simpler, streamlined cartoon image for Mr. Peanut

Practice Test 6

12. <u>Instead of</u> using elaborate computer-generated
     A

effects, the science fiction series <u>employing</u>
                          B

<u>compelling acting</u> and clever plot twists to hold <u>its</u>
     C   D

viewers' attention. <u>No error</u>
                  E

13. Following a disastrous first debate, the incumbent

<u>to decide</u> to regain <u>his lead</u> by embarking on a tour
   A   B

<u>of the states</u> where the polls showed him to be
   C

<u>extremely vulnerable</u>. <u>No error</u>
          D   E

14. <u>Although</u> Sam's articles <u>have begun</u> to appear on a
     A   B

popular technology blog, this new publicity

<u>however</u> has not brought him either steady income
   C

<u>or</u> personal fulfillment. <u>No error</u>
D   E

15. While Stephen's science fair display was

<u>more elaborate</u> and colorful <u>than Elizabeth,</u>
     A   B

it soon <u>became clear</u> that Elizabeth's project
         C

<u>was superior</u> in its use of hard statistics and
   D

scientific method. <u>No error</u>
                E

16. Despite the enormous and enduring

<u>popularity against</u> zombie movies, there
     A

has been little interest in creating <u>an entire</u>
                         B

zombie-themed amusement park, <u>since</u> such a
                          C

destination <u>would not attract</u> the large family
             D

audience needed for robust profits. <u>No error</u>
                          E

17. Like <u>the tragicomedies of</u> Luigi Pirandello, the
          A

plays of Samuel Beckett <u>present</u> their audiences
                    B

with a world <u>that is</u> devoid of certainty, <u>yet</u> often
            C   D

full of ironic comedy. <u>No error</u>
                E

18. <u>Unless you</u> read <u>at least</u> two or three newspaper
     A   B

columns every day, it will be impossible <u>for one</u>
                                C

to develop <u>a real awareness</u> of foreign policy.
         D

<u>No error</u>
E

19. <u>Contrasting</u> the fairly cautious architects of early
     A

nineteenth-century America, <u>architects later</u> in the
                      B

century created edifices <u>that</u> wildly incorporated
               C

styles <u>from England</u>, Rome, and Japan. <u>No error</u>
        D   E

20. With characters such as dashing samurai and

stately aristocrats, <u>the films</u> of Akira Kurosawa
                     A

transport <u>its viewers</u> to vibrant eras <u>that</u> have
          B   C

<u>passed into</u> Japanese history and folklore. <u>No error</u>
 D   E

21. The philosophical system <u>developed by</u> Arthur
                        A

Schopenhauer, <u>who influencing</u> generations of
                  B

European <u>writers and artists</u>, posits that humanity is
             C

driven by a relentless "will" that <u>continually</u> seeks
                           D

satisfaction. <u>No error</u>
            E

22. <u>Among</u> the greatest poems <u>written in</u> Old English
    A   B

<u>are</u> the epic narrative *Beowulf*, <u>which</u> tells the story
C   D

of a warrior civilization plagued by vengeful

monsters. <u>No error</u>
        E

23. Pastoral literature, a genre <u>which</u> depicts simplified
                        A

<u>and idealized</u> countryside lifestyles, <u>were</u> popular
     B   C

in the late sixteenth century in <u>both</u> England and
                         D

Spain. <u>No error</u>
       E

24. <u>Anyone who</u> wants to succeed <u>as an entrepreneur</u>
    A   B

would do well <u>to read</u> business magazines, such as
           C

Forbes and *The Economist*, that <u>provides</u>
                        D

information on investments and startup industries.

<u>No error</u>
 E

25. Ms. Cleary and her neighbor Ms. Gosford <u>decided</u>
                                   A

to begin a local anti-bullying campaign

<u>after witnessing</u> <u>her son</u> being mercilessly teased
           B   C

<u>by</u> his classmates. <u>No error</u>
 D   E

26. It is common for colleges <u>to welcome</u>
                      A

accepted students to on-campus events, <u>including</u>
                            B

home games, <u>theatrical performances</u>, and even
                C

<u>commencement ceremonies</u>. <u>No error</u>
       D   E

27. The estates <u>of both</u> Thomas Jefferson and George
            A

Washington <u>has become</u> popular tourist attractions,
            B

though it is unlikely that <u>either</u> of these <u>sites rivals</u>
                   C   D

Colonial Williamsburg in popularity. <u>No error</u>
                          E

28. The <u>felling</u> of ancient redwoods in the Pacific
       A

Northwest <u>has been welcomed</u> by some
            B

environmentalists; <u>however</u>, others claim that
              C

<u>they are</u> not an acceptable way of dealing with
   D

ecological problems. <u>No error</u>
               E

29. Every time Mr. Burrell and his son take a trip

<u>to the local barbershop</u>, <u>he</u> cannot <u>help feeling</u> a
        A   B   C

sensation of simultaneous dread, anticipation,

<u>and excitement</u>. <u>No error</u>
    D   E

(1) For many years, electric and partially-electric cars have been marketed as a means of both protecting the environment and saving money. (2) This is true of one of today's bestselling automobiles, the "hybrid" gas-and-electric Toyota Prius, which can average a remarkable 50 miles per gallon; most cars that run purely on gasoline average 20 to 25 miles per gallon. (3) However, consumers are now purchasing hybrid and electric cars for a new reason: they want to make a statement about luxury and prestige. (4) Designed to be both efficient and beautiful, a new generation of environmentally-safe cars has captured the imagination of the public.

(5) One of the most remarkable environmentally safe luxury cars is the Tesla Model S. (6) The Model S is the brainchild of businessman and engineer Elon Musk, and it was designed to run purely on electric energy. (7) The car is easy to handle and has very precise steering, but its dramatic exterior styling and finely proportioned body makes it a work of art.

(8) Another car that competes with the Model S is the BMW i8, the latest offering from one of the world's most respected automakers. (9) This BMW model appeared in the action movie *Mission Impossible: Ghost Protocol*; indeed, the i8 even looks like an exciting superhero car. (10) Yet there is one big downside to breakthrough automobiles such as these: price. (11) It is known that the Tesla Model S can sell for well over $50,000, and the price with the BMW i8, I believe, has been set for over $100,000.

30. The best way to describe the relationship between sentence 2 and sentence 1 is that sentence 2

(A) anticipates a reader's possible response to a divisive claim made in sentence 1
(B) highlights statistical data that disproves the main assertion of sentence 1
(C) introduces a viewpoint that contradicts the apparent bias of sentence 1
(D) presents new details to expand upon the anecdote offered in sentence 1
(E) provides a specific example that substantiates an idea set forward in sentence 1

31. In context, which is the best version of the underlined portion of sentence 3 (reproduced below)?

However, consumers are now purchasing hybrid and electric cars for <u>a new reason: they want to</u> make a statement about luxury and prestige.

(A) (as it is now)
(B) new reason; which is because buyers want to
(C) a new reason: these consumers wanting to
(D) a new reason. These cars
(E) a new reason, wanting to

32. Which of the following is the best sentence to insert at the beginning of the second paragraph?

(A) Recent consumer reports on safety and reliability, however, indicate that hybrid cars may be much faultier than traditional models.
(B) In order for hybrid cars to enter the mainstream, massive consumer reeducation must be implemented and the public must be convinced that these purchases are cost-efficient.
(C) Despite these developments, most manufacturers seem to be forced into choosing either fuel efficiency or luxury, never both.
(D) At present, car buyers have many options from which to choose, but only a select few automobiles meet the criteria of both fuel efficiency and luxury.
(E) It is no surprise that cars that feature luxurious trimmings and advanced technologies are also cars with the extremely precise steering and handling.

33. In context, which of the following best combines sentences 5 and 6?

(A) The Tesla Model S is one of the most remarkable environmentally safe luxury cars and is the brainchild of businessman and engineer Elon Musk, even though it was designed to run purely on electric energy.

(B) One of the most remarkable environmentally safe luxury cars is the Tesla Model S, which was designed by businessman and engineer Elon Musk to run purely on electric energy.

(C) One of the most remarkable environmentally safe luxury cars, the Tesla Model S, as the brain child of businessman and engineer Elon Musk, it was designed by him to run purely on electric energy.

(D) One of the most remarkable environmentally safe luxury cars is the Tesla Model S, the brainchild of businessman and engineer Elon Musk, being designed to run purely on electric energy.

(E) The Tesla Model S, because it is one of the most remarkable environmentally safe luxury cars, is the brainchild of businessman and engineer Elon Musk and was designed to run purely on electric energy.

34. In context, which version of sentence 8 (reproduced below) would most effectively introduce the last paragraph?

Another car that competes with the Model S is the BMW i8, the latest offering from one of the world's most respected automakers.

(A) (As it is now)

(B) Musk's endeavors in new technology have not been limited solely to automobiles; indeed, he is the founder of the much-publicized space exploration company SpaceX.

(C) On the other hand, the BMW i8 has brought a completely unprecedented set of aesthetic principles to automotive design.

(D) Because of stark competition from longer-lived automakers such as BMW, the Tesla Model S has not received the same praise as another hybrid car, the i8.

(E) To make luxury alternative-energy cars acceptable to a mainstream audience, BMW designed its i8 with the film industry in mind.

35. In context, which of the following revisions would NOT improve sentence 11 (reproduced below)?

It is known that the Tesla Model S can sell for well over $50,000, and the price with the BMW i8, I believe, has been set for over $100,000.

(A) Delete "It is known that".

(B) Change "can sell" to "may sell".

(C) Change "and" to "while".

(D) Delete "I believe".

(E) Change "price with" to "price of".

STOP

If you finish before time is called, you may check your work on this section only. Do not turn to any other section in the test.

SECTION 2
Time–10 minutes
14 Questions

1. Each winter, nearly a billion monarch <u>butterflies migrating south</u> to central Mexico where the pine and *oyamel* firs provide a warm enough haven for survival.

   (A) butterflies migrating south
   (B) butterflies that migrate south
   (C) butterflies on their southward migration
   (D) butterflies migrates south
   (E) butterflies migrate south

2. Flora's sparkling intellect and bright <u>smile makes</u> her the most worthy candidate for prom queen.

   (A) smile makes
   (B) smile making
   (C) smile make
   (D) smile is what make
   (E) smile that make

3. Though he had a troubled personal life, *Tonight Show* host Johnny Carson displayed impressive wit, impeccable timing, and <u>extensive knowledge that amazed his viewers</u>.

   (A) extensive knowledge that amazed his viewers
   (B) knowing what to amaze his viewers with extensively
   (C) amazement from his knowledge that was extensive
   (D) viewers were amazed by his extensive knowledge
   (E) knowledge, viewers found this extensive and amazing

4. <u>Called "urban ecology," anthropologists believe that a new branch of study is needed</u> to understand how cities function.

   (A) Called "urban ecology," anthropologists believe that a new branch of study is needed
   (B) Anthropologists believe that a new branch of study, called "urban ecology," is needed
   (C) Called "urban ecology," study for a new branch that anthropologists need is believed
   (D) Anthropologists, calling it "urban ecology," believe in the need for a new branch while studying
   (E) Anthropologists call it "urban ecology," they believe that this new branch of study is needed

5. Ms. Jameson, who passes her spare time making fanciful lithographs of cats dressed up in human clothes, <u>have rented out a booth at the summer art fair in her hometown in the hopes of selling a few of her creations</u>.

   (A) have rented out a booth at the summer art fair in her hometown in the hopes of selling a few of her creations
   (B) a booth at the summer art fair in her hometown has rented it in the hopes of selling a few of her creations
   (C) with a few of her creations, she has rented out a booth at the summer art fair in her hometown in the hopes of selling
   (D) with a booth at the summer art fair in her hometown, she was renting in the hopes of selling a few of her creations
   (E) has rented out a booth at the summer art fair in her hometown in the hopes of selling a few of her creations

6. Everyone should <u>keep track of their spending habits</u> to avoid going into debt.

   (A) keep track of their spending habits
   (B) make sure that they keep track of their spending habits
   (C) keep track of his or her spending habits
   (D) keep track of one's spending habits
   (E) keep track of your spending habits

7. <u>If you want to invest money in an online stock trading account</u>, you should be prepared to incur a transaction fee of at least a few dollars for every transaction you make.

   (A) If you want to invest money in an online stock trading account
   (B) For you investing money in an online stock trading account
   (C) Without having you invest money in an online stock trading account
   (D) If you had an online stock trading account, with money being invested
   (E) For an online stock trading account, where you are investing money

8. <u>It does not garner the same critical respect as some traditional modes of painting and sculpture, nonetheless folk art</u> is still popular among museum-goers and, increasingly, among affluent collectors of contemporary art.

   (A) It does not garner the same critical respect as some traditional modes of painting and sculpture, nonetheless folk art
   (B) While it does not garner the same critical respect as some traditional modes of painting and sculpture, folk art
   (C) Not garnering the same critical respect as some traditional modes of painting and sculpture, however folk art
   (D) Folk art, although it does not garner the same critical respect as some traditional modes of painting and sculpture, nonetheless it
   (E) Because it does not garner the same critical respect as some traditional modes of painting and sculpture, folk art nonetheless

9. The teachers at the private school were advised to write grades and comments not in red, which students associate with aggression and punishment, <u>but they must be made with a more soothing color such as blue or green.</u>

   (A) but they must be made with a more soothing color such as blue or green
   (B) but in a more soothing color such as blue or green
   (C) but a more soothing color such as blue or green is how they should be made
   (D) but made with blue or green, which are two more soothing colors
   (E) but make them with blue, green, or more soothing colors

10. In her essay for medical school, Danielle positioned herself as <u>a truly cosmopolitan applicant, her interests range from classic Chinese literature to community service.</u>

    (A) a truly cosmopolitan applicant, her interests range from classic Chinese literature to community service
    (B) a truly cosmopolitan applicant whose interests range from classic Chinese literature to community service
    (C) a truly cosmopolitan applicant, her interests from classic Chinese literature to community service
    (D) a truly cosmopolitan applicant, with interests between classic Chinese literature and community service
    (E) a truly cosmopolitan applicant, although her interests from classic Chinese literature to community service

11. Found on the islands of Indonesia, the Komodo Dragon is a carnivorous reptile that can grow up to ten feet long <u>though they are known to eat</u> deer, wild pigs, and even water buffalo.

    (A) though they are known to eat
    (B) which makes it known to eat
    (C) and is known to eat
    (D) and they are known as eating
    (E) as well as eating

12. Those who praise public readings of essays <u>claim that they help for bringing</u> new voices to the attention of a wider public, to say nothing of prominent publicists and magazine editors.

    (A) claim that they help for bringing
    (B) claim that this helps if you want to bring
    (C) would claim that they help to bring
    (D) claimed that it is helpful, besides bringing
    (E) claim that these events help to bring

13. Without the financial assistance provided on a regular basis by her parents and the staunch support of her network of friends, the young model's ambition to build a portfolio of runway shows and appearances in advertisements would never have been fulfilled.

(A) the young model's ambition to build a portfolio of runway shows and appearances in advertisements would never have been fulfilled

(B) building a portfolio of runway shows and appearances in advertisements is an ambition that would never have been fulfilled by the young model

(C) the young model, whose ambition was to build a portfolio of runway shows and appearances in advertisements, would have never fulfilled it

(D) the young model would never have fulfilled her ambition to build a portfolio of runway shows and appearances in advertisements

(E) the young model's ambition, which was building a portfolio of runway shows and appearances in advertisements, this would never have been fulfilled

14. To automatically dismiss poetry that is intentionally difficult is rejection of some of the most influential and edifying poems of the past hundred years.

(A) is rejection of some of the most influential and edifying poems of the past hundred years

(B) is to reject some of the most influential and edifying poems of the past hundred years

(C) is rejecting some of the most influential and edifying poems of the past hundred years

(D) is, in the past hundred years, a rejection of some of the most influential and edifying poems

(E) is what it means to reject some of the poems that are the most influential and edifying of the past hundred years

STOP
If you finish before time is called, you may check your work on this section only.
Do not turn to any other section in the test.

(ANSWERS ON PAGE 209)

Chapter 21
PRACTICE TEST 7

SECTION 1
Time–25 minutes
35 Questions

1. The dermatologist explained that, by seeking shade and wearing sunscreen, you can avoid premature wrinkles and sunspots.

(A) and wearing sunscreen
(B) and to wear sunscreen
(C) or having sunscreen worn
(D) or sunscreen is worn
(E) or you could wear sunscreen

2. During the massive floods of 2002, professionals at the Prague Zoo, in tranquilizing the tigers to evacuate cages at risk of flooding.

(A) Prague Zoo, in tranquilizing the tigers to
(B) Prague Zoo, they tranquilized the tigers
(C) Prague Zoo tranquilized the tigers in order to
(D) Prague Zoo tranquilized the tigers, and to
(E) Prague Zoo, who tranquilized the tigers to

3. Carl Linnaeus, who received most of his higher education at Uppsala University, and is most famous for creating a universal system for naming organisms.

(A) and is most famous for creating
(B) is most famous for creating
(C) and who is most famous for having created
(D) is despite this most famous as creating
(E) he is most famous for creating

4. In 1821 Nathaniel Hawthorne was sent to Bowdoin College in Brunswick, Maine, there he met future poet Henry Wadsworth Longfellow.

(A) there he met future poet Henry Wadsworth Longfellow
(B) meeting future poet Henry Wadsworth Longfellow
(C) when he met future poet Henry Wadsworth Longfellow
(D) that was where he met future poet Henry Wadsworth Longfellow
(E) where he met future poet Henry Wadsworth Longfellow

5. King Henry IV, who famously converted to Catholicism to appease his French subjects, and he enacted the Edict of Nantes in order to encourage religious tolerance.

(A) who famously converted to Catholicism to appease his French subjects, and he enacted
(B) famously converted to Catholicism to appease his French subjects, he also enacted
(C) who famously converted to Catholicism to appease his French subjects, enacting
(D) who famously converted to Catholicism to appease his French subjects, he enacted
(E) who famously converted to Catholicism to appease his French subjects, enacted

6. The 1773 protest famously dubbed the Boston Tea Party, as a watershed event it marked the culmination of American frustration with unfair taxation.

(A) Boston Tea Party, as a watershed event
(B) Boston Tea Party was a watershed event
(C) Boston Tea Party was a watershed event because
(D) Boston Tea Party a watershed event because
(E) Boston Tea Party a watershed event in that

7. Exploration of deep sea ecosystems have led to the discovery of unusual survival strategies among species living without light or oxygen.

(A) have led to the discovery of
(B) are proven to have led to the discovery with
(C) has led to the discovery of
(D) is proven to have led to the discovery from
(E) led to them discovering

8. By the time Janice arrived at the airport, she <u>has already missed</u> her flight to Morocco.

(A) has already missed
(B) had already missed
(C) would already miss
(D) will already miss
(E) was already missing

9. The weather report predicted a massive thundershower, <u>and it made the principal cancel</u> the outdoor picnic.

(A) and it made the principal cancel
(B) therefore, the principal canceling
(C) this being the reason why the principal canceled
(D) so the principal canceled
(E) as a result, the principal would cancel

10. <u>While taking the MCAT, a qualifying test for those wishing to enter medical school, Hank's desk collapsed and completely disrupted his focus.</u>

(A) While taking the MCAT, a qualifying test for those wishing to enter medical school, Hank's desk collapsed and completely disrupted his focus.
(B) Hank's desk collapsed while taking the MCAT, a qualifying test for those wishing to enter medical school, and completely disrupted his focus.
(C) Hank's desk collapsed and completely disrupted his focus while taking the MCAT, a qualifying test for those wishing to enter medical school.
(D) While Hank was taking the MCAT, a qualifying test for those wishing to enter medical school, his desk collapsed and completely disrupted his focus.
(E) While Hank was at his desk taking the MCAT, a qualifying test for those wishing to enter medical school, collapsing and completely disrupting his focus.

11. Strangely enough, there is a plaque in a public park in Bramborough, Delaware, honoring Captain Chet, <u>dying at the impressive age of sixty-three as a domesticated potbellied pig.</u>

(A) dying at the impressive age of sixty-three as a domesticated potbellied pig
(B) dying at the impressive age of sixty-three, and had also been a domesticated potbellied pig
(C) a domesticated potbellied pig that died at the impressive age of sixty-three
(D) dying at the impressive age of sixty-three and being a domesticated potbellied pig
(E) from dying at the impressive age of sixty-three unlike a domesticated potbellied pig

21   **21**   **21**   **21**

Unauthorized copying or
reuse of any part of this
page is illegal.

21   **21**   **21**

Practice Test 7

12. <u>A new franchise</u>, Pepperoni Pete's Pan Pizza,
     A

<u>has been experiencing</u> phenomenal growth;
       B

already, the company <u>has built popular</u>
              C

<u>restaurants on</u> twenty seven states. <u>No error</u>
   D   E

13. One <u>need not</u> worry about the future <u>if one</u> does
      A   B

not care <u>whether</u> <u>they will</u> eventually enter a
       C   D

competitive and prestigious profession.

<u>No error</u>
  E

14. To deal with irregularities <u>in class attendance</u>,
                    A

Professor Firestone <u>has instituted</u> a new policy;
              B

now, each student <u>needing to</u> sign an attendance
             C

sheet <u>when</u> class begins, and a second form when
      D

class ends. <u>No error</u>
        E

15. Our public speaking teacher, Mrs. Sassoon,

<u>said</u> that we <u>should always</u> try <u>and speak</u>
 A   B   C

authoritatively about a given subject, regardless

of whether <u>we</u> really possess expert knowledge.
          D

<u>No error</u>
  E

16. <u>Had</u> the sound of the <u>alarm clock's</u> beeping not
   A   B

awakened him when <u>they did</u>, he <u>would have</u>
            C   D

missed the important interview. <u>No error</u>
                    E

17. Based <u>in Brooklyn</u>, the intellectual magazine *n+1*
      A

<u>has built</u> <u>a devoted readership</u> over the past
  B   C

seven years, although some commentators

dismiss its articles as petty and <u>presumptuously</u>.
                           D

<u>No error</u>
  E

18. A versatile <u>cooking ingredient</u>, the avocado is also
           A

<u>a food that</u> imparts remarkable health benefits;
   B

it is believed that eating one avocado a day

<u>can help you</u> burn body fat even <u>without exercise</u>.
    C   D

<u>No error</u>
  E

19. <u>Even though</u> he <u>is revered</u> by scholars of twentieth-
    A   B

century culture, artist Mark Rothko is probably

less respected and admired <u>by the general</u> public
                   C

than <u>the paintings of</u> Norman Rockwell. <u>No error</u>
     D   E

20. The main difference <u>between his</u> business plan and
              A

mine is that, while his <u>focuses on</u> accelerating
               B

short-term profits, mine is designed <u>to increasing</u>
                       C

efficiency <u>and productivity</u> over the long term.
         D

<u>No error</u>
  E

21. <u>From winning</u> a seat on the school board,
     A

Bruce <u>was forced</u> to give intensive thought to
        B

community issues that, <u>before his appointment,</u>
                     C

he <u>had only considered</u> in passing. <u>No error</u>
      D   E

22. The <u>amount of</u> attention that <u>is lavished</u> on issues
         A   B

<u>surrounding</u> contemporary social media sites is far
C

greater <u>than healthcare</u>. <u>No error</u>
        D   E

23. In order to get a job <u>at</u> a major publishing
                 A

company, you do not need a specialized

degree in English <u>or literature</u>; some publishing
                B

houses, in fact, <u>prefer</u> to hire editors
             C

<u>with marketing backgrounds</u>. <u>No error</u>
     D   E

24. Mr. Cartwright <u>had</u> no trouble winning more votes
            A

<u>than any other</u> candidate, but his margin of victory
 B

in the City Council <u>election were</u> not large enough
              C

to be considered <u>a true mandate</u>. <u>No error</u>
        D   E

25. Angela is <u>clearly dissatisfied</u> with the career
         A

paths that her sons <u>have chosen</u>, yet she refrains
            B

<u>from explicit</u> criticizing her sons because
    C

she wants to avoid offending <u>them</u>. <u>No error</u>
                D   E

26. The governor <u>attempted</u> to justify a series of
          A

recent tax <u>increases with</u> stating that the funds
        B

<u>would be used</u> to make essential repairs
C

<u>to the state's</u> roads, train lines, and public parks.
   D

<u>No error</u>
E

27. Animals such as the wombat and the chinchilla,

<u>which</u> can be quite cantankerous <u>in real life,</u>
A   B

<u>has</u> frequently been transformed into adorable,
C

friendly mascots <u>for popular sports teams</u>.
               D

<u>No error</u>
E

28. I was given the go-ahead to <u>precede with</u> my
                   A

teaching, under the conditions that <u>I adhere</u> closely
                     B

to my department's syllabus <u>and carefully</u> check
               C

<u>all the facts</u> in my lectures. <u>No error</u>
 D   E

29. <u>Unless</u> the university reforms <u>its student housing</u>
   A   B

policies immediately, it is likely <u>that the campus</u>
                    C

government <u>will organize</u> a boycott of the recent
         D

dorm and roommate selection events. <u>No error</u>
                     E

21 21 21 21 21 21 21

Unauthorized copying or
reuse of any part of this
page is illegal.

(1) Herman Melville's massive novel *Moby-Dick* was written and published in the middle of the nineteenth century. (2) Since this time, this book will reach the undisputed status of a classic, even though very few people have read Melville's 500-page story from front to back. (3) Most of the people who have read it are college professors and students in American literature courses. (4) The answer is ironic, yet most people are infinitely fascinated by books that they may never have the time to read.

(5) *Moby-Dick* is only one example of an immensely long and difficult book that intrigues a huge group of readers. (6) People react similarly to novels like Leo Tolstoy's *Anna Karenina* and Thomas Mann's *The Magic Mountain*, both of these books are over seven hundred pages long, a number that can both drive potential readers away and grab their attention. (7) But these aren't even the most extreme cases. (8) Even fewer readers will attempt to read Samuel Richardson's novel *Clarissa* (a stunning 1500 pages) or Marcel Proust's masterpiece *In Search of Lost Time* (a staggering 3200 pages). (9) Nobody would doubt that these are great works of literature, but many has a logical fear that reading this much would be, to rephrase Proust's title, "time lost."

30. In context, what is the best way to deal with sentence 2?

(A) Leave it as it is.
(B) Delete the sentence.
(C) Use "but" at the end of the sentence 2 to link it with sentence 3.
(D) Place it after sentence 3.
(E) Change "will reach" to "has reached".

31. Which of the following sentences would be best to insert between sentence 3 and sentence 4?

(A) So why does Melville's intimidating novel enjoy such fame?
(B) How did we lose the endurance needed to read long novels?
(C) Without the emphasis on small bits of information that social media has fostered, would the length of *Moby-Dick* even be a problem?
(D) Why did Melville, despite his awareness of the growing stature of the huge novel, later devote his energies to the short story?
(E) Is there a single reason that explains Melville's remarkable popularity in college curriculums?

32. Of the following, which is the best revision for sentence 4 (reproduced below)?

The answer is ironic, yet most people are infinitely fascinated by books that they may never have the time to read.

(A) Change "is" to "was".
(B) Change "yet" to a colon.
(C) Change "that they" to "and they".
(D) Change "they" to "he or she".
(E) Change "to read" to "in reading".

33. Which revision is the most necessary for the underlined portion of sentence 6 (reproduced below)?

People react similarly to novels like Leo Tolstoy's Anna Karenina *and Thomas Mann's* The Magic Mountain, *both of these books are over seven hundred pages long, a number that can both drive potential readers away and grab their attention.*

(A) (as it is now)
(B) and Thomas Mann's *The Magic Mountain*. Both of these books are
(C) and Thomas Mann's *The Magic Mountain*; and both of these books are
(D) and Thomas Mann's *The Magic Mountain*, whose books are
(E) but Thomas Mann's *The Magic Mountain* was a book that was

34. Of the following, what is the best way to deal with sentence 8?

(A) Leave it as it is.
(B) Delete the sentence.
(C) Insert the phrase "Because of this" at the beginning.
(D) Move it to the beginning of the second paragraph.
(E) Move it to the end of the essay as a final statement.

35. In context, which of the following is the best version of the underlined portion of sentence 9 (reproduced below)?

Nobody would doubt that these are great works of literature, but many has a logical fear that *reading this much would be, to rephrase Proust's title, "time lost."*

(A) literature, yet many would have a logical fear which
(B) literature; although many logically fearing that
(C) literature, many have had a logical fear in which
(D) literature, but many fear the logic that
(E) literature, but many have a logical fear that

STOP

**If you finish before time is called, you may check your work on this section only.
Do not turn to any other section in the test.**

21   21   21   21   21   21   21

Unauthorized copying or reuse of any part of this page is illegal.

SECTION 2
Time–10 minutes
14 Questions

1. Ralph Waldo Emerson, who wrote many essays that challenged convention, <u>are widely recognized</u> as the father of Transcendentalism.

   (A) are widely recognized
   (B) have wide recognition
   (C) they are widely recognized
   (D) he is widely recognized
   (E) is widely recognized

2. <u>There was twelve students from the senior class that</u> received nominations this year for the state's academic and athletic excellence award.

   (A) There was twelve students from the senior class that
   (B) There were twelve students, and they were in the senior class that
   (C) Twelve students from the senior class
   (D) Twelve students, from the senior class, were those that
   (E) Of the senior class, it was twelve students who

3. If anyone crosses the line by running too far or falling past the marked boundary, <u>you will be disqualifying</u> the rest of the team in the relay race.

   (A) you will be disqualifying
   (B) he or she will disqualify
   (C) you will disqualify
   (D) they will disqualify
   (E) they will be disqualifying

4. Since the concert tickets are for general admission only, <u>attendees looking for a good seat that will afford him or her clear views of the performers</u> will have to arrive early to beat the crowd.

   (A) attendees looking for a good seat that will afford him or her clear views of the performers
   (B) attendees looking for a good seat that will afford them clear views of the performers
   (C) attendees looking for good seats that will afford him or her clear views of the performers
   (D) attendees looking for good seats that will afford clear views of the performers
   (E) attendees are looking for good seat that will afford them clear views of the performers

5. The Habsburg Empire, which was part of the Holy Roman Empire, <u>is considered by some historians to have been</u> one of the most important royal houses of Europe.

   (A) is considered by some historians to have been
   (B) and is considered by some historians to have been
   (C) it was considered by some historians to have been
   (D) and considered by some historians to have been
   (E) is considered by some historians being

6. <u>Today his paintings are worth millions, and</u> he is one of the most celebrated modern Italian painters, Amadeo Modigliani lived his life in relative obscurity and modesty.

   (A) Today his paintings are worth millions, and
   (B) In spite of today his paintings being worth millions when
   (C) His paintings are worth millions today although
   (D) Though today his paintings are worth millions, yet
   (E) Though today his paintings are worth millions and

7. The modern month of July takes its name from Julius Caesar, the legendary Roman politician; <u>despite this, August takes its name from Caesar's eventual successor</u>, the Roman emperor Augustus.

   (A) despite this, August takes its name from Caesar's eventual successor
   (B) August in contrast has a name which is Caesar's eventual successor
   (C) moreover, August takes its name from Caesar's eventual successor
   (D) August, which was named after Caesar's eventual successor
   (E) Caesar's eventual successor had August taken for his name

8. <u>Author Karl Ove Knausgaard's six-volume autobiographical novel *My Struggle* has been hailed</u> as one of the most ambitious and thought-provoking writers working today.

   (A) Author Karl Ove Knausgaard's six-volume autobiographical novel *My Struggle* has been hailed
   (B) Karl Ove Knausgaard, author of the six-volume autobiographical novel *My Struggle*, has been hailed
   (C) Author Karl Ove Knausgaard and his six-volume autobiographical novel *My Struggle* have been hailed
   (D) In contrast to his six-volume autobiographical novel *My Struggle*, author Karl Ove Knausgaard has been hailed
   (E) Whereas his six-volume novel *My Struggle* is autobiographical, author Karl Ove Knausgaard is being hailed

9. The firm's attempt to hire individuals from more diverse age groups was thwarted <u>because of discovering that many</u> of the youngest applicants lacked sufficient workplace experience.

   (A) because of discovering that many
   (B) when many made the discovery
   (C) by the discovery that many
   (D) by it having been discovered that many
   (E) when they discovered that many

10. Those who wish to pursue a career in government may find that successfully running a political campaign requires stellar public speaking skills, the ability to garner support from special interest groups, and <u>to have enough publicity to achieve name recognition among voters</u>.

    (A) to have enough publicity to achieve name recognition among voters
    (B) having enough publicity to achieve name recognition for voters
    (C) they also need enough publicity to achieve name recognition among voters
    (D) enough publicity to achieve name recognition among voters
    (E) with enough publicity to achieve name recognition among voters

11. The doctor explained to the patient that the symptoms of strep throat are quite similar <u>to the whooping cough</u>.

    (A) to the whooping cough
    (B) to that of the whooping cough
    (C) as those of the whooping cough
    (D) than the whooping cough
    (E) to those of the whooping cough

12. Constructed in the 1920s, the 130-foot statue of Christ the Redeemer in Rio de Janiero, Brazil, is perhaps the largest and most famous outdoor sculpture in the world, <u>until the statue of Christ the King in Poland was actually taller</u>.

    (A) until the statue of Christ the King in Poland was actually taller
    (B) with the statue of Christ the King in Poland actually being taller
    (C) until the statue of Christ the King in Poland would be actually taller
    (D) despite the statue of Christ the King and its being actually taller
    (E) although the statue of Christ the King in Poland is actually taller

13. Franklin Delano Roosevelt's tenure as United States president lasted 12 years, longer than <u>did any other</u> United States president.

(A) did any other
(B) that of any
(C) that of any other
(D) those of any other
(E) any other

14. Refuting the widespread assumption that a life in academia is poor training for involvement in public affairs, <u>a new group of candidates rose, and have proven that college professors</u> can win primary runoffs and even gubernatorial elections.

(A) a new group of candidates rose, and have proven that college professors
(B) a new group of candidates has arisen to prove that college professors
(C) new candidates have rose in a group to prove that college professors
(D) a new group of candidates, because they are college professors, have risen
(E) a new group of candidates are both rising as well as proving that college professors

STOP

**If you finish before time is called, you may check your work on this section only.
Do not turn to any other section in the test.**

(ANSWERS ON PAGE 209)

Chapter 22
PRACTICE TEST 8

Practice Test 8

SECTION 1
Time–25 minutes
35 Questions

1. Rather than allowing himself to be overcome by despair, Herman decided to make new friends, join new activities, <u>and he will become better at speaking in public</u>.

   (A) and he will become better at speaking in public
   (B) as well as becoming better at speaking in public
   (C) and become better at speaking in public
   (D) and despite this he became a better public speaker
   (E) in contrast to becoming better as a public speaker

2. Henry James Sr. fathered two famous sons, the philosopher William James and <u>Henry James who was a novelist</u>; however, he also wrote original tracts of his own on religious belief and supernatural phenomena.

   (A) Henry James who was a novelist
   (B) the novelist Henry James
   (C) Henry James, as a novelist
   (D) a novelist, who was Henry James
   (E) in contrast a novelist, Henry James

3. The continent of Australia was originally a landmass <u>attached to the coast of Antarctica; in contrast, from this position</u> it moved northward over a period of millions of years.

   (A) attached to the coast of Antarctica; in contrast, from this position
   (B) which, from its position on the coast of Antarctica, attached itself and
   (C) which, though once attached to the coast of Antarctica, from this position
   (D) attached to the coast of Antarctica, later from this position
   (E) attached to the coast of Antarctica; from this position

4. Many students are attracted to college courses in art history and philosophy, yet in the years after college, few graduates <u>found gainful employment in them</u>.

   (A) found gainful employment in them
   (B) are finding gainful employment there
   (C) find gainful employment in these fields
   (D) will find gainful employment in that field
   (E) find these fields to be a gainful employment

5. A new science fiction film is based on <u>a terrifying scenario despite it not being entirely implausible</u>: a massive tremor takes place deep in the Earth's core, causing every volcano on the planet to erupt simultaneously.

   (A) a terrifying scenario despite it not being entirely implausible
   (B) a scenario which is terrifying and it is also not entirely implausible as well
   (C) a scenario, in which it is terrifying though not entirely implausible
   (D) a terrifying though not entirely implausible scenario
   (E) a terrifying scenario, and in addition to this it is not entirely implausible

6. Started as a single-location college in 2007, the Computer Career Institute has gradually expanded; now, working adults can earn degrees in engineering, web design, and business administration <u>and they enroll at one of the Institute's many campuses</u>.

   (A) and they enroll at one of the Institute's many campuses
   (B) by enrolling at one of the Institute's many campuses
   (C) who enroll at one of the Institute's many campuses
   (D) as well as enrollment at one of the Institute's many campuses
   (E) because they are enrolled, the Institute having many campuses

7. Although oil, vinegar, and parmesan cheese are the basic components of any Caesar salad dressing, some gourmet versions <u>use special ingredients such as diced anchovies and crushed pine nuts</u>.

   (A) use special ingredients such as diced anchovies and crushed pine nuts
   (B) which use special ingredients, for instance diced anchovies and crushed pine nuts
   (C) have special ingredients, such as diced anchovies and crushed pine nuts, which are used in them
   (D) were using special ingredients, which are diced anchovies and crushed pine nuts
   (E) with diced anchovies and crushed pine nuts being used as the special ingredients

8. The atypical chronology and strange subject matter of Quentin Tarantino's films <u>promises an originality for its presentation</u> that is not seen in most movies.

   (A) promises an originality for its presentation
   (B) promise an originality for its presentation
   (C) is the reason for why they promise to be original and
   (D) are promises for its originality
   (E) promise an original presentation

9. Despite her extensive background in literature and criticism, Mrs. Prentice came to be regarded as an unfair English teacher as a result of her willingness <u>of penalizing her students for minuscule grammar mistakes</u>.

   (A) of penalizing her students for minuscule grammar mistakes
   (B) because she penalized her students for minuscule grammar mistakes
   (C) to penalize her students for minuscule grammar mistakes
   (D) which penalized her students for minuscule grammar mistakes
   (E) when minuscule grammar mistakes caused her to penalize her students

10. <u>We always assumed</u> that owning a summer house in Tuscany would be the perfect escape from the hustle and bustle of New York City, we were disappointed to discover that our vacation home lacked the most basic modern amenities.

   (A) We always assumed
   (B) Always having assumed
   (C) Always had we assumed
   (D) Always when we assumed
   (E) We had always assumed

11. For a business, opening many branches within a small area can be an effective means of <u>projecting an appearance of popularity, and also they increase brand awareness among passing pedestrians</u>.

   (A) projecting an appearance of popularity, and also they increase brand awareness among passing pedestrians
   (B) having an appearance of popularity projected, and this has increased brand awareness among passing pedestrians
   (C) projecting an appearance, which is to have popularity and also to increase brand awareness among passing pedestrians
   (D) projecting an appearance of popularity and among passing pedestrians increasing brand awareness
   (E) projecting an appearance of popularity and of increasing brand awareness among passing pedestrians

22 · 22 · 22 · 22 · 22 · 22 · 22 · 22

Unauthorized copying or
reuse of any part of this
page is illegal.

12. A well-organized publishing company <u>can produce</u>
                                              A

informative guidebooks simply by <u>being hired</u> a
                                        B

few knowledgeable <u>freelance writers</u> and two <u>or</u>
                            C   D

three highly-motivated nonfiction editors. <u>No error</u>
                                             E

13. The members of the theatrical troupe kept

<u>his or her</u> faces fixed in unchanging expressions
A

and <u>relied on</u> gesture, <u>dance</u>, and expressive
        B   C

lighting <u>to convey</u> emotion. <u>No error</u>
          D   E

14. <u>The ambassador</u> attempted to give <u>effective and</u>
      A   B

succinct answers to the reporters' inquiries,

<u>also he was unable</u> to respond coherently to
          C

<u>questions about</u> the recent hostage crisis. <u>No error</u>
     D   E

15. <u>Active during</u> the first half of the twentieth century,
     A

director Sergei Eisenstein <u>was much more</u>
                            B

innovative <u>than</u> many of the other <u>Russian films</u>
           C   D

of his era. <u>No error</u>
            E

16. <u>Although</u> Jeffrey's unusually high confidence
    A

<u>has allowed him</u> to excel as an employee,
     B

<u>they have</u> also caused a few of his <u>less ostentatious</u>
    C   D

co-workers to resent his personality. <u>No error</u>
                               E

17. <u>By being</u> the owner of a Mexican food franchise,
    A

Mr. Dominguez <u>must travel</u> regularly to
                B

Southwestern states <u>such as</u> New Mexico and
                 C

Arizona to make sure that his restaurants <u>are</u> in
                                 D

good working order. <u>No error</u>
                E

18. Director Julie Taymor <u>is known</u> not only <u>for her</u>
                     A   B

film versions <u>of respected</u> Shakespeare plays
             C

<u>and also</u> for her popular Broadway spectaculars,
   D

including *The Lion King*. <u>No error</u>
                   E

19. In a series of recent comments, author Junot Díaz

<u>criticized</u> creative writing programs <u>and called for</u>
   A   B

a more <u>cultural and ethnic</u> inclusive approach to
          C

teaching <u>contemporary fiction</u>. <u>No error</u>
       D   E

20. <u>Those who</u> believe that video games can have
    A

<u>a beneficial and</u> therapeutic influence <u>cite</u> a variety
    B   C

of studies, some <u>of whom were</u> published in only
                D

the past five years, to support their assertions.

<u>No error</u>
  E

21. Over the last <u>several years</u>, the average vocabulary
　　　　　　　　A
<u>score on</u> standardized tests <u>for fifth graders</u>
　B　　　　　　　　　　　　　　C
<u>have decreased</u> by approximately twenty percent.
　　　D
<u>No error</u>
　E

22. <u>Yearning</u> to relive her childhood, Samantha
　A
<u>returned</u> to her <u>old house in</u> Oregon and found the
　B　　　　　　C
hallway where she <u>had took</u> her very first steps.
　　　　　　　　D
<u>No error</u>
　E

23. The Chinese were quite possibly the first

<u>to manufacture</u> gunpowder <u>in large quantities</u>,
　A　　　　　　　　　　　　　B
but <u>the English</u> were the first to craft weapons
　　　C
of war <u>that depended</u> on gunpowder. <u>No error</u>
　　　　D　　　　　　　　　　　E

24. The three-toed sloth, which <u>spends</u> most of its life
　　　　　　　　　　　　　A
suspended <u>from jungle trees</u>, moves so little that
　　　　　B
moss will often begin <u>to grow</u> on <u>their fur</u>.
　　　　　　　　　C　　　D
<u>No error</u>
　E

25. Upon relocating to Minneapolis, Dwight

<u>discovered</u> that Merguez sausage, <u>which</u> had
　A　　　　　　　　　　　B
long been <u>one of his</u> favorite foods, <u>were</u>
　　　　　C　　　　　　　D
not available in any of the local supermarkets.

<u>No error</u>
　E

26. If we <u>do not provide</u> better training in practical

　　　　A
skills, <u>we will</u> soon be living in a country where
　　　　B
college-educated students <u>are incapable</u> of
　　　　　　　　　　　　　C
managing their finances and <u>they depend on</u> their
　　　　　　　　　　　　　D
parents for money. <u>No error</u>
　　　　　　　　E

27. Although Mark had intended his <u>remarks as</u>
　　　　　　　　　　　　　A
compliments, Dorothy <u>interpreted</u> <u>his comments</u> on
　　　　　　　B　　　　C
her huge new house as <u>implicit criticism</u> of
　　　　　　　　　D
her spending habits. <u>No error</u>
　　　　　　　E

28. My parents <u>recently</u> purchased a car for both
　　　　A
<u>my older brother and I</u>, although <u>I suspect that</u>
　B　　　　　　　　　　C
I will be using the car much <u>more frequently</u> on
　　　　　　　　　D
account of the long commute to my part-time job.

<u>No error</u>
　E

29. Jogging <u>on a daily</u> basis can help you <u>both</u>
　　　　A　　　　　　　　B
lose excess weight through exercise and

<u>have prevented</u> the risk of heart disease
　C
<u>later in</u> life. <u>No error</u>
　D　　　　E

Practice Test 8

(1) It is hard to imagine some shows on television with different names. **(2)** Can anybody imagine calling *Sesame Street* anything other than *Sesame Street*? **(3)** Yet odd enough, the popular children's program almost aired under another series title, and could all too easily have been loved and remembered as something else. **(4)** Their working title, which was very close to being approved by the producers, was *1-2-3 Avenue B*.

(5) As longtime viewers will remember, *Sesame Street* features actors, puppets, and sometimes animation, all of it is set in welcoming urban settings that recall Manhattan. **(6)** As commentators have noted, the name *1-2-3 Avenue B* was rejected because it could marginalize viewers outside of New York City. **(7)** Other titles, such as *Fun Street* and *The Video Classroom*, was also considered. **(8)** The decision to go with *Sesame Street* was made very much at the last minute, but the name stuck. **(9)** It recalls the saying "Open sesame!" and indicates that the show is somewhere where magical and adventurous things are possible.

(10) *Sesame Street* aired in 1969, and one of its first skits seems to reference the story of its naming. **(11)** A promotional video features puppets in a business meeting in which they cannot think of an appropriate name for their show.

30. Which of the following phrases would most appropriately be inserted at the beginning of sentence 2?

   (A) On other hand,
   (B) Therefore,
   (C) Ironically,
   (D) Notwithstanding,
   (E) For example,

31. Which of the following is the best revision of the underlined portion of sentence 3 (reproduced below)?

   Yet odd enough, the popular children's program almost aired under another series title, and could all too easily have been loved and remembered as something else.

   (A) Yet oddly enough, the popular children's program
   (B) And odd enough, the popularity of this children's program
   (C) The popularity of this children's program oddly enough
   (D) Although odd enough, this popular children's program
   (E) But strangely enough, the popularity of *Sesame Street*

32. In context, which of the following revisions is the most necessary for the underlined portion of sentence 4 (reproduced below)?

   Their working title, which was very close to being approved by the producers, was 1-2-3 Avenue B.

   (A) Their working titles, which were
   (B) Its working title, which was
   (C) Their working title, it was
   (D) As a result, a working title, which was
   (E) *Sesame Street*, which was the working title

33. Of the following, which is the best revision for the underlined portion of sentence 5 (reproduced below)?

   As longtime viewers will remember, Sesame Street *features actors, puppets, and sometimes animation,* all of it is set in welcoming *urban settings that recall* Manhattan.

   (A) all set in welcoming
   (B) all was set in welcoming
   (C) all would be set in welcoming
   (D) all setting themselves in welcoming
   (E) all set beside welcoming

34. Of the following, which is the most necessary revision for sentence 7 (reproduced below)?

Other titles, such as Fun Street *and* The Video Classroom*, was also considered.*

(A) Replace "such as" with "like".
(B) Replace "and" with a semicolon.
(C) Omit "also".
(D) Change "was" to "were".
(E) Change "considered" to "to be considered".

35. Which of the following would make the most logical final sentence for the essay?

(A) But *Sesame Street* was not unique in its predicament; *Barney and Friends*, a children's program that first aired in the 1990s, suffered a similar problem.
(B) As the show grew in popularity, the cast of puppets came to include Big Bird and Oscar the Grouch, both of whom were created by Jim Henson.
(C) Despite its clever references, this promotional video was reshot several times at the behest of adolescent psychologists, who were convinced that interaction between puppets and humans would be confusing for children.
(D) Despite new forms of competition, including computer-animated cartoons and children's programming from the United Kingdom, *Sesame Street* continues to draw in new devotees year after year.
(E) Finally, they arrive at the series name, *Sesame Street*, which would be respected by viewers young and old for the next 45 years.

STOP
If you finish before time is called, you may check your work on this section only.
Do not turn to any other section in the test.

22 **22** **22** **22** **22** **22** **22**

Unauthorized copying or reuse of any part of this page is illegal.

SECTION 2
Time–10 minutes
14 Questions

1. Current reports indicate that increased sightings of great white sharks, one of the ocean's apex predators, <u>they have</u> occurred due to the migration of the sharks' primary prey, seals.

    (A) they have
    (B) have
    (C) they had
    (D) having
    (E) this had

2. Independence Day in America is regularly commemorated <u>with such an event as</u> firework shows, barbecues, and parades.

    (A) with such an event as
    (B) with an event such as
    (C) with such events as
    (D) in such events like
    (E) in an event like that of

3. Jonathan Wong, a native of Jamaica who is the descendant of Chinese immigrants, <u>have always spoken with a Patois inflection that reveals his culturally mixed origins</u>.

    (A) have always spoken with a Patois inflection that reveals his culturally mixed origins
    (B) and has always spoken with a Patois inflection, which reveals his culturally mixed origins
    (C) revealing his culturally mixed origins by speaking with a Patois inflection
    (D) always speaks with a Patois inflection that reveals his culturally mixed origins
    (E) always he was speaking with a Patois inflection that revealed his culturally mixed origins

4. While studying abroad in Europe, <u>it became clear to Simón Bolívar that independence from Spanish sovereignty was necessary for the people of South America</u>.

    (A) it became clear to Simón Bolívar that independence from Spanish sovereignty was necessary for the people of South America
    (B) Simón Bolívar realized that independence from Spanish sovereignty will have been a necessity for the people of South America
    (C) the Spanish sovereignty made it clear to Simón Bolívar that the people of South America needed independence from them
    (D) Simón Bolívar realized that independence from Spanish sovereignty would be necessary for the people of South America
    (E) the Spanish sovereignty clarified Simón Bolívar's necessity for independence for the people of South America

5. <u>Within the confines of their room and without regard for their behavior, protocol was abandoned by the spies.</u>

    (A) Within the confines of their room and without regard for their behavior, protocol was abandoned by the spies.
    (B) The spies abandoned protocol within the confines of their room, and they were having no regard for their behavior either.
    (C) The protocol of the spies, abandoned within the confines of their room, was behaved without regard.
    (D) Although without regard for their behavior within the confines of their room, their protocol was abandoned by the spies.
    (E) The spies, within the confines of their room and without regard for their behavior, abandoned protocol.

6. <u>Pears, of which there are several varieties based on color, texture, and geographic origin, are best when eaten raw yet this will maximize their nutritional value.</u>

(A) Pears, of which there are several varieties based on color, texture, and geographic origin, are best when eaten raw yet this will maximize their nutritional value.

(B) With several varieties based on colors, textures, and geographic origins, the nutrients in pears are best maximized when eaten raw.

(C) Known to have several varieties based on color, texture, and geographic origin, pears are best when eaten raw, so that their nutritional value is maximized.

(D) There are several varieties of pears; based on color, texture, and geographic origin, their nutrients would be maximized if eaten raw.

(E) There are several varieties of pears based on color, texture, and geographic origin, even though nutrients are maximized for them when eaten raw.

7. Because I grew up in Paris, <u>it was only when I studied abroad in America that I noticed how different European universities are when compared to those of America.</u>

(A) it was only when I studied abroad in America that I noticed how different European universities are when compared to those of America

(B) I did not notice the differences between European universities and American universities until I studied abroad in America

(C) when in America I studied abroad and I only noticed how different European universities were from those of America

(D) I noticed how different European and American universities studying abroad were when I went to America

(E) European universities were indeed different from American ones as I studied abroad in America

8. Robollita, a hearty Italian soup made from bread and vegetables, <u>are popular in the city of Florence, where rich yet unsalted bread</u> is an essential ingredient in many dishes.

(A) are popular in the city of Florence, where rich yet unsalted bread

(B) are popular in the city of Florence; its bread is rich yet unsalted because it

(C) is popular in the city of Florence, where rich yet unsalted bread

(D) both popular in the city of Florence, even though rich yet unsalted bread

(E) is popular in the city of Florence, which is the case when rich yet unsalted bread

9. The twine bracelets and embroidered satchel <u>resembles that of the traditional Mexican culture</u> that predated the inclusion of Spanish influence.

(A) resembles that of the traditional Mexican culture

(B) resemble those of the traditional Mexican culture

(C) resembles the one that in Mexican culture is traditional

(D) resembles traditional Mexican culture

(E) resemble Mexico in its traditions

10. The rules of the club are firm: any member who cannot recite the club's pledge, <u>along with their code of honor, will be forced to give up their club membership.</u>

(A) along with their code of honor, will be forced to give up their club membership

(B) and they must recite the code of honor or be forced to give up their club membership

(C) also reciting the code of honor, will be forced to give up his or her club membership

(D) will be forced to give up their club membership, along with reciting the club's code of honor

(E) along with its code of honor, will be forced to give up his or her club membership

Practice Test 8

11. Once regarded as <u>little more than a highly efficient vehicle</u>, commercial airplanes have evolved over the decades to offer luxuries such as reclining seats, entertainment systems, and high-quality cuisine.

   (A) little more than a highly efficient vehicle
   (B) a highly efficient vehicle and little more than this
   (C) little more than highly efficient vehicles
   (D) highly efficient vehicles when there was little more
   (E) little more than a vehicle whose efficiency was high

12. A philosophical zombie is a form of argument used in thought experiments <u>where the theories of behaviorism and materialism are systematically disproven</u>.

   (A) where the theories of behaviorism and materialism are systematically disproven
   (B) in which the theories of behaviorism and materialism are systematically disproven
   (C) that have disproved systematically the theories of behaviorism and materialism
   (D) that have disproved theories, these are systematic behaviorism and materialism
   (E) having systematically disproved theories like behaviorism and materialism

13. James M. Cain's novel *Mildred Pierce* was adapted to both a 1945 film and a 2011 television series <u>because of the same name</u>.

   (A) because of the same name
   (B) of the same name
   (C) within the same name
   (D) for the same name
   (E) despite the same name

14. Several determined freshman students <u>participating in the relay race, their spirit was not diminished</u> despite the competition from the upper class students.

   (A) participating in the relay race, their spirit was not diminished
   (B) participating in the relay race, their spirit never diminishing
   (C) participating in the relay race, and their spirit never diminished
   (D) participated in the relay race, their spirit never diminishing
   (E) participated in the relay race, and their spirit never diminishing

STOP
If you finish before time is called, you may check your work on this section only.
Do not turn to any other section in the test.

Chapter 23
PRACTICE TEST 9

Practice Test 9

SECTION 1
Time–25 minutes
35 Questions

1. Fitness trainers suggest that before beginning your workout, the trainee should consider stretching his or her muscles to increase blood circulation.

   (A) the trainee should consider stretching his or her muscles
   (B) one should consider stretching one's muscles
   (C) trainees should consider stretching their muscles
   (D) your muscles, which should be stretched by you, are
   (E) you should consider stretching your muscles

2. Mr. Andrews, who wanted to teach his students about the importance of having specific arguments in their papers, and illustrated his point by comparing the sharp point of an axe to the blunt end of a baseball bat.

   (A) and illustrated his point by comparing the sharp point of an axe to the blunt end of a baseball bat
   (B) an illustration of his point by comparing the sharp point of an axe to the blunt end of a baseball bat
   (C) and illustrated his point to compare the sharp point of an axe to the blunt end of a baseball bat
   (D) illustrates his point where he was comparing the sharp point of an axe to a baseball bat
   (E) illustrated his point by comparing the sharp point of an axe to the blunt end of a baseball bat

3. Astronomers, whose research depends very little on abstract speculation, relies on physics and mathematics to explore the material universe beyond the Earth's atmosphere.

   (A) relies on physics and mathematics to explore
   (B) physically and mathematically relies on an exploration of
   (C) rely on physics and mathematics to explore
   (D) to explore, relying on physics and mathematics involving
   (E) exploring, by relying on physics and mathematics

4. Between the three beverages offered, Regina preferred the coconut water because it reminded her of her childhood in Fiji.

   (A) Between the three beverages offered, Regina preferred
   (B) Of the three beverages offered, Regina preferred
   (C) For the three offered beverages, Regina preferred
   (D) Between the three offerings which were beverages, Regina could prefer
   (E) In between the three offered beverages, Regina was preferring

5. The sport of javelin-throwing does not put its participants in direct danger, but damage to one's bones and ligaments can result if proper throwing techniques are not rigorously observed.

   (A) The sport of javelin-throwing does not put its participants in direct danger
   (B) Even though the sport of javelin-throwing does not put its participants in direct danger
   (C) The sport of javelin-throwing, which does not put its participants in direct danger
   (D) In javelin-throwing, participants are not put in direct danger by it as a sport
   (E) Although a sport, participants in javelin-throwing are not put in direct danger

6. Significant technological advances in biological medicine have led to remarkable cost-efficient practices where it is possible to provide much needed medical attention to even the most impoverished areas.

   (A) practices where it is possible to provide
   (B) practices in which it can possibly provide
   (C) practices by making it possible to provide
   (D) practices that make it possible despite providing
   (E) providing practices, especially making the possibility for

7. A college professor who loses the love of his life in a car accident, <u>the novel *A Single Man* has a protagonist who struggles</u> to resume a normal life.

  (A) the novel *A Single Man* has a protagonist who struggles
  (B) the novel's protagonist, which is *A Single Man*, struggles
  (C) *A Single Man* is a novel in which the protagonist struggles
  (D) the protagonist of the novel *A Single Man* struggles
  (E) the novel *A Single Man* has a protagonist whose struggle is

8. Forced to recall hundreds of thousands of automobiles with defective brakes, <u>a huge loss of both revenue and public esteem greeted the once-venerated car company</u>.

  (A) a huge loss of both revenue and public esteem greeted the once-venerated car company
  (B) the once-venerated car company was greeted with a huge loss of both revenue and public esteem
  (C) it was a once-venerated car company greeted by a huge loss of both revenue and public esteem
  (D) the car company was once venerated, a huge loss of both revenue and public esteem greeting it
  (E) revenue and public esteem, which were involved in a huge loss, greeted the once-venerated car company

9. The similarity between the primacy of emotion in Impressionist works and <u>how much reality is distorted by Abstract Expressionist works</u> is not obvious to the untrained eye, yet these features reflect a common philosophy of art.

  (A) how much reality is distorted by Abstract Expressionist works
  (B) the reality is distorted by Abstract Expressionist works
  (C) the distortion of reality in Abstract Expressionist works
  (D) those of Abstract Expressionist work
  (E) there being a distortion of reality by Abstract Expressionist works

10. Bronze, the amalgam of copper and tin, was used in early blacksmithing for weapons such as spears and <u>swords, but would eventually be replaced as the sturdier iron</u>.

  (A) swords, but would eventually be replaced as the sturdier iron
  (B) swords; however, it would eventually be replaced by sturdier iron
  (C) swords, yet iron would replace this because of its sturdiness
  (D) swords, which would be replaced by the sturdiness of iron
  (E) swords, eventually replacing this with iron because it is sturdy

11. Even though they were initially irked by the speed and accuracy exercises mandated by their teacher, the students in the fifth-grade computer skills course later <u>understand the necessity with these seemingly tedious assignments</u>.

  (A) understand the necessity with these seemingly tedious assignments
  (B) will understand these seemingly tedious assignments and when they are a necessity
  (C) came to understand the necessity of these seemingly tedious assignments
  (D) have the understanding, and these seemingly tedious assignments will be a necessity
  (E) understanding these seemingly tedious assignments, since they were necessary

12. The <u>plays of</u> Anton Chekhov <u>can fill</u> an audience
       A   B
with a variety of emotions, <u>including joy</u>, anxiety,
                                              C
<u>and they are sad</u>. <u>No error</u>
          D   E

13. Unlike <u>Roberto</u>, Martha's short story eschews the
              A
trendy experimental <u>techniques of</u> the past few
                              B
years and delivers <u>its narrative</u> in an unembellished
                            C
<u>yet moving</u> fashion. <u>No error</u>
      D   E

14. One of the most popular inventions <u>to emerge from</u>
                                                    A
the telecommunications <u>startup are</u> a software
                                B
program that allows <u>its users</u> to sample
                            C
newly-released CDs <u>for only</u> a small monthly
                            D
charge. <u>No error</u>
              E

15. In order <u>to improve</u> your reading comprehension,
                  A
<u>you can</u> perform simple daily activities
    B
like <u>skimming</u> newspaper columns,
        C
<u>leisure time put aside</u> for novels and short stories,
          D
and writing down difficult new words. <u>No error</u>
                                                    E

16. Now <u>on sale</u> at the mall <u>is</u> several *haute couture*
          A   B
dresses, all of them made by the top designers
whose works <u>have been featured</u> during Fashion
                        C
Week <u>in New York City</u>. <u>No error</u>
          D   E

17. If you approach difficult writing tasks
<u>calm and confidently</u>, you <u>will have</u> no trouble
          A   B
<u>writing</u> effective papers within the deadlines
    C
<u>your teacher</u> has set. <u>No error</u>
      D   E

18. George <u>has worked</u> <u>as a chemical engineer</u> for over
                A   B
fifteen years, <u>now he is</u> abandoning this
                    C
well-paying career <u>and</u> using his savings to open
                            D
his own video arcade. <u>No error</u>
                              E

19. The news of the presidential election
<u>was particularly</u> upsetting to <u>Jack and I</u>, <u>since</u>
          A   B   C
we had traveled all over our neighborhood
<u>and</u> had campaigned for the candidate who lost.
D
<u>No error</u>
    E

20. <u>Less interested</u> in <u>receiving</u> lavish presents <u>as in</u>
          A   B   C
showing her own values of thoughtfulness and
generosity, Linda gave <u>each guest</u> at her graduation
                              D
a small bag of party favors. <u>No error</u>
                                    E

21. <u>The attempt</u> to institute Esperanto as a universal
        A
mode of communication <u>has been</u> widely regarded as
                              B
unsuccessful, though <u>there are still</u> enthusiasts
                            C
<u>to this</u> language all over the world. <u>No error</u>
    D   E

22. While many people <u>have qualms</u> about
A
living in absolute solitude, Simon <u>is always</u>
B
<u>happiest</u> during the two months he spends every
C
summer <u>for a remote</u> cabin in the woods of
D
Vermont. <u>No error</u>
E

23. <u>Because it</u> instinctively hunts and kills cobra
A
snakes, the mongoose <u>are</u> regularly fed and
B
domesticated <u>by Indian villagers</u> who wish
C
<u>to exterminate</u> poisonous reptiles. <u>No error</u>
D   E

24. <u>There are</u> two primary reasons for Walter
A
Mondale's landslide <u>loss to</u> Ronald Reagan in the
B
1984 presidential election: widespread <u>satisfaction</u>
C
with Reagan's administration <u>with Mondale's</u> own
D
flaws as a campaigner. <u>No error</u>
E

25. Unlike many of his contemporaries,

<u>who prized</u> a cosmopolitan education, Henry David
A
Thoreau <u>believed that</u> to remain close to
B
home <u>was accessing</u> an abundance
C
<u>of philosophical insight</u>. <u>No error</u>
D   E

26. <u>Apparently unhappy</u> with the recent publicity
A
<u>efforts for</u> the bake sale, Mrs. Adler called Rupert,
B
Natalie, <u>and I</u> into her office and encouraged us to
C
rethink <u>our present strategy</u>. <u>No error</u>
D   E

27. Nature artist John James Audubon's <u>depictions of</u>
A
rabbits, otters, <u>and other small mammals</u> are
B
extremely popular, though these <u>images are</u>
C
certainly not as well-known <u>as birds</u>. <u>No error</u>
D   E

28. One recent recipient <u>from the Nobel Prize</u> in
A
Economics <u>has argued</u> that small consumer goods
B
companies can thrive in countries <u>dominated by</u>
C
only <u>a handful</u> of major retail stores. <u>No error</u>
D   E

29. Exposed to relentless downpours <u>which have</u> only
A
a few packets of food, the passengers of

the lifeboat <u>urgently hoped</u> that a ship
B
<u>would appear</u> in the vicinity <u>within a day</u> at most.
C   D
<u>No error</u>
E

(1) I have always enjoyed traditional ballet, participating even in a few dance recitals as I was growing up. **(2)** Despite the fact that it took me a long time, though, before I experienced the world of non-classical dance after seeing my first modern, experimental dance performance this past summer. **(3)** For my birthday, I was given a ticket to the Alvin Ailey Dance Company. **(4)** They were performing just a brief train ride away from my hometown, with a repertoire of works based on both African-American traditions and modern theories of movement and dynamism.

(5) It took me a little while to understand exactly how an Alvin Ailey piece is meant to be interpreted; contrasting to a traditional long ballet such as *Swan Lake*, there is neither a storyline nor a definable character. **(6)** Soon though, it became clear to me that everything in an Ailey routine has a clear purpose. **(7)** Each set of dances refer to historical or cultural forces, or to ideas from society and religion.

(8) Perhaps the most incredible expression of this kind of art is the dance composition *Revelations*, which is regarded as an Alvin Ailey masterpiece. **(9)** In its different movements, *Revelations* conjures up references to the sacrament of Baptism, to evil and sin, and to the pleasures of worship and community. **(10)** The finale is large and grand, but also seems like a moment of true joy and redemption.

30. Which of the following is the most necessary revision for the underlined portion of sentence 1 (reproduced below)?

    I have always enjoyed traditional ballet, participating even in a few dance recitals as I was growing up.

    (A) and I even participated in a few dance recitals while I was growing up
    (B) having participated in a few dance recitals as I grow up
    (C) even though I participated in a few dance recitals as I was growing up
    (D) participating in a few dance recitals after I grew up
    (E) with participation in a few dance recitals growing up

31. In context, the underlined portion of sentence 2 (reproduced below) could be best revised in which of the following ways?

    Despite the fact that it took me a long time, though, before I experienced the world of non-classical dance after seeing my first modern, experimental dance performance this past summer.

    (A) It had taken me a long time, however, until I would experience
    (B) Without ever having experienced for a long time
    (C) It was a long time before my experience in
    (D) Before a long time, I experienced this
    (E) Though it took me a long time, I eventually experienced

32. Of the following, which is the most necessary revision for sentence 5 (reproduced below)?

    It took me a little while to understand exactly how an Alvin Ailey piece is meant to be interpreted; contrasting to a traditional long ballet such as Swan Lake*, there is neither a storyline nor a definable character.*

    (A) Omit "meant to be".
    (B) Replace the semicolon with "and".
    (C) Change "contrasting to" to "unlike".
    (D) Insert "yet" after the semicolon.
    (E) Change "nor" to "but".

33. Which of the following revisions would best improve sentence 7 (reproduced below)?

Each set of dances refer to historical or cultural forces, or to ideas from society and religion.

(A) Change the comma to a semicolon.
(B) Change "refer" to "refers".
(C) Change "or to" to "but also".
(D) Omit "ideas from".
(E) Insert "Despite this" at the beginning of the sentence.

34. Sentence 9 in the passage is best described as

(A) an introduction of a new topic to question the reader's assumptions
(B) a controversial opinion about the uses of art
(C) an explanation of a previously mentioned composition
(D) an ambivalent response to a dance
(E) an obscure reference that is designed to confuse the reader

35. In context, where should the following sentence be placed to best improve the passage?

Revelations celebrates physical movement and the emotive powers of art in ways that would make any dance enthusiast proud.

(A) At the beginning of the last paragraph
(B) Between sentences 3 and 4
(C) Between sentences 6 and 7
(D) Before sentence 10
(E) At the end of the last paragraph

STOP
If you finish before time is called, you may check your work on this section only.
Do not turn to any other section in the test.

SECTION 2
Time–10 minutes
14 Questions

1. Janet, who loves throwing spring-themed tea parties, gave all of her guests gift bags with homemade lollipops shaped like tulips.

   (A) gave all of her guests gift bags with homemade lollipops shaped like tulips
   (B) she gave all of her guests gift bags with homemade lollipops shaped like tulips
   (C) gave all of her guests, shaped like tulips, gift bags with homemade lollipops
   (D) gave all of her guests gift bags, they were shaped like tulips with homemade lollipops
   (E) giving all of her guests gift bags with homemade lollipops shaped like tulips

2. The delicate arrangement of flowers inside the late Mrs. Peel's shadowboxes is a reminder for her children that her memory will live on forever.

   (A) is
   (B) are
   (C) being
   (D) have been
   (E) having been

3. The California Roll, a popular item that reimagines traditional Japanese cuisine, became wildly popular in the 1980s because of its recognizable name and for being distinctive about its taste.

   (A) and for being distinctive about its taste
   (B) but was distinctive as it tasted
   (C) for it was a distinctive taste
   (D) and the taste was making it distinctive
   (E) and its distinctive taste

4. Neanderthals and Cro-Magnons are important in differences between them: Neanderthals were stronger, while Cro-Magnons were more adept at using tools and thinking strategically.

   (A) Neanderthals and Cro-Magnons are important in differences between them
   (B) The difference is between Neanderthals and Cro-Magnons, which are important
   (C) Having an important difference were Neanderthals, as well as Cro-Magnons
   (D) There were important differences between Neanderthals and Cro-Magnons
   (E) The differences between Neanderthals and Cro-Magnons, having been important

5. Realizing that a yacht would have limited resale value, the lottery winnings were instead used by Ursula on long-term stock investments and much-needed repairs to her family home.

   (A) the lottery winnings were instead used by Ursula on long-term stock investments and much-needed repairs to her family home
   (B) Ursula instead used her lottery winnings on long-term stock investments and much-needed repairs to her family home
   (C) Ursula used her lottery winnings on long-term stock investments, also she had made much needed repairs on her family home instead
   (D) the lottery winnings, instead of long-term stock investments and much-needed repairs to her family home, were used by Ursula
   (E) Ursula, in contrast to her lottery winnings, used long-term stock investments and much-needed repairs to her family home

194

6. Chaim Potok's book *The Chosen* <u>will be successfully adapted to a four-actor drama, and it has toured</u> several playhouses in New York and the surrounding suburbs.

 (A) will be successfully adapted to a four-actor drama, and it has toured
 (B) would be successfully adapted to a four-actor drama because they are touring
 (C) has been a successful four-actor drama, which is adapted despite touring
 (D) being a successful four-actor drama, it has been adapted and it tours
 (E) was successfully adapted as a four-actor drama, which went on to tour

7. Speaking like a true leader, <u>Christian used personal anecdotes, wise quotations, and powerful flights of emotion when he delivered his valedictorian speech to the class.</u>

 (A) Christian used personal anecdotes, wise quotations, and powerful flights of emotion when he delivered his valedictorian speech to the class
 (B) Christian, using personal anecdotes, wise quotations, and powerful flights of emotion and then he delivered his valedictorian speech to the class
 (C) the valedictorian speech, delivered by Christian, used personal anecdotes, wise quotations, and powerful flights of emotion for the class
 (D) personal anecdotes, wise quotations, and powerful flights of emotion were used by Christian to deliver his valedictorian speech to the class
 (E) Christian's valedictorian speech was delivered to the class using personal anecdotes, wise quotations, and powerful flights of emotion

8. The land snail, like all other shelled gastropod mollusks, <u>retract into their shells</u> when threatened by predators.

 (A) retract into their shells
 (B) and retracts into its shell
 (C) retracts into its shell
 (D) retracting into their shells
 (E) has retracted into its shell

9. With the aim of generating more followers, the online television production <u>company included social media advertisements during their scheduled programming so that viewers could simply click and follow while watching the shows you enjoy.</u>

 (A) company included social media advertisements during their scheduled programming so that viewers could simply click and follow while watching the shows you enjoy
 (B) company included social media advertisements during its scheduled programming so that viewers could simply click and follow while watching the shows they enjoy
 (C) company will often include social media advertisements that viewers, while watching the shows they enjoy, could simply click and followed during their scheduled programming
 (D) company included social media advertisements during its scheduled programming, viewers as a result simply clicked and followed while watching the shows they enjoyed
 (E) company includes viewers who enjoy their scheduled programming by simply clicking and following the social media advertisements contrasting to the shows

10. Many asserted that the decreased population of rats in the city's sewers indicated that the water <u>toxicity, which had risen as the result of improperly maintained residential plumbing and in the plumbing of commercial areas.</u>

 (A) toxicity, which had risen as the result of improperly maintained residential plumbing and in the plumbing of commercial areas
 (B) toxicity had risen as the result of improperly maintained residential and commercial plumbing
 (C) toxicity is rising as the result of improperly maintained residential plumbing and there is commercial plumbing also
 (D) toxicity, being risen as the result of both improperly maintained residential and commercial plumbing
 (E) toxicity, it will continue to rise as the result of the improper maintenance of residential and commercial plumbing

11. Some early hip-hop music, which included songs by ensembles such as Grandmaster Flash and the Furius Five, <u>were known for calling attention to the social problems</u> that faced American cities in the 1980s and 1990s.

   (A) were known for calling attention to the social problems
   (B) was known by calling attention to the social problems
   (C) was a social problem that was known for calling attention
   (D) was known to call attention to the social problems
   (E) were the same as calling attention to a social problem

12. <u>There is a belief that one catches a cold simply from being cold, but in reality their symptoms come from a virus, not the temperature.</u>

   (A) There is a belief that one catches a cold simply from being cold, but in reality their symptoms come from a virus, not the temperature.
   (B) There is a belief that one catches a cold simply from being cold, but in reality, cold symptoms come from a virus, not from the temperature.
   (C) There is a belief that we catch a cold simply from being cold, in reality, this is symptomatic of a virus and not your temperature.
   (D) One catches a cold, it is believed, simply from being cold, but in reality its symptoms come from a virus contrasted to the temperature.
   (E) It is believed that a cold can be caught simply from being cold, but with the temperature a cold can come from a virus.

13. Cinco de Mayo celebrates Mexico's victory over the French at the Battle of Puebla, <u>and many people assume it to be Mexico's independence</u>.

   (A) and many people assume it to be Mexico's independence
   (B) but many people assume it to be Mexico's independence
   (C) not, as many people assume, Mexico's independence
   (D) not what many people assume, being Mexico's independence
   (E) yet many people assume it from Mexico's independence

14. To face your innermost fears is <u>a valuable first step taken toward building traits of honesty and resilience</u> that can last a lifetime.

   (A) a valuable first step taken toward building traits of honesty and resilience
   (B) building traits of honesty and resilience through a valuable first step
   (C) to take a valuable first step toward building traits of honesty and resilience
   (D) taking a valuable first step toward building traits of honesty and resilience
   (E) a trait that is a valuable first step taken toward being honest and resilient

STOP
**If you finish before time is called, you may check your work on this section only.
Do not turn to any other section in the test.**

(ANSWERS ON PAGE 210)

Chapter 24

PRACTICE TEST 10

SECTION 1
Time–25 minutes
35 Questions

1. The students at the summer camp were required to make a choice: either they could participate in the kayaking trip <u>and they could go rock climbing</u>, but not both.

   (A) and they could go rock climbing
   (B) nor they could go rock climbing
   (C) as well, they could go rock climbing
   (D) or rocks could be climbed by them
   (E) or they could go rock climbing

2. Following a heated argument with his neighbor, Mr. Nussbaum <u>driving away in his car</u> and was not seen until almost a week later.

   (A) driving away in his car
   (B) will drive away in his car
   (C) drove away in his car
   (D) his car was driving away
   (E) and his car, they drove away

3. <u>The flying buttress, which was a hallmark of the architecture of the Middle Ages, and was used</u> to create stunning effects in French cathedrals in Rheims, Chartres, and Paris.

   (A) The flying buttress, which was a hallmark of the architecture of the Middle Ages, and was used
   (B) A hallmark of the architecture of the Middle Ages, the flying buttress was used
   (C) The flying buttress was a hallmark of the architecture of the Middle Ages, it was used
   (D) The flying buttress, which as architecture in the Middle Ages is one of its hallmarks, was used
   (E) Although a hallmark of architecture in the Middle Ages, the flying buttress was used

4. Before her death in 1941, <u>novelist Virginia Woolf has composed</u> a series of essays on important literary subjects, such as the connection between an author's personal identity and his or her larger historical situation.

   (A) novelist Virginia Woolf has composed
   (B) Virginia Woolf would be a novelist by
   (C) Virginia Woolf, who was a novelist, is composing
   (D) novelist Virginia Woolf composed
   (E) Virginia Woolf has composed as a novelist

5. <u>Believed to have paved the way for future African-American actors, Sidney Poitier in his films highlight</u> the ongoing struggle to dismantle vicious stereotypes.

   (A) Believed to have paved the way for future African-American actors, Sidney Poitier in his films highlight
   (B) Sidney Poitier is believed to have paved the way for future African-American actors, his films highlight
   (C) The films of Sidney Poitier, believed to have paved the way for future African-American actors, highlight
   (D) Believing that the way was paved for future African-American actors, Sidney Poitier's films highlight
   (E) Sidney Poitier's films, in addition to believing that he paved the way for future African-American actors, highlighting

6. Educators have long debated whether the goal of children's literature should be to encourage values such as obedience and patience <u>or to unleash the imaginative potential of young readers</u>.

   (A) or to unleash the imaginative potential of young readers
   (B) or unleashing young readers with an imaginative potential
   (C) or young readers, whose imaginative potential is unleashed
   (D) or the potential, for young readers, of imagination being unleashed
   (E) despite the unleashing of the imaginative potential of young readers

Practice Test 10

7. <u>After he was winning the Nobel Prize for Literature, the nonprofit stage company decided to showcase Eugene O'Neill's works as part of the summer lineup.</u>

   (A) After he was winning the Nobel Prize for Literature, the nonprofit stage company decided to showcase Eugene O'Neill's works as part of the summer lineup.
   (B) The nonprofit stage company decided to showcase the works of Eugene O'Neill, who won the Nobel Prize for Literature, in its summer lineup.
   (C) Eugene O'Neill's works, which won the Nobel Prize for Literature, was showcased by the nonprofit stage company in its summer lineup.
   (D) The nonprofit stage company decided to showcase Eugene O'Neill as part of the summer lineup; and those works won the Nobel Prize for Literature.
   (E) They won the Nobel Prize for Literature, and the works of Eugene O'Neill became a part of the summer lineup by the nonprofit stage company because of this.

8. <u>Each year, an annual report indicates</u> the growth and geographic spread of red wolf populations in North America.

   (A) Each year, an annual report indicates
   (B) An annual report indicates
   (C) Yearly reports indicate annually
   (D) A report indicates that yearly
   (E) Annually, a yearly report indicates

9. Bike riding in the early 1990s grew more popular in urban areas <u>than</u> the 1980s.

   (A) than
   (B) than rural areas in
   (C) than they did in
   (D) despite the bike riding of
   (E) than did bike riding in

10. Annoyed by Gregory's tendency to obsess over small details to the detriment of larger project goals, <u>he was informed by his employers</u> that he would need to adhere to their standards or his contract would be terminated.

   (A) he was informed by his employers
   (B) information came from his employers
   (C) they, his employers, notified Gregory
   (D) his employers informed him
   (E) Gregory's information from his employers was

11. Affluent business executives contribute to charities for <u>a variety of reasons: while some of them simply hope to earn tax deductions individually, there is for others a genuine desire to do good.</u>

   (A) a variety of reasons: while some of them simply hope to earn tax deductions individually, there is for others a genuine desire to do good
   (B) a variety of reasons, from simply hoping to earn tax deductions individually to others that have a genuine desire to do good
   (C) a variety of reasons: while some of these individuals simply hope to earn tax deductions, others have a genuine desire to do good
   (D) a variety of reasons, from a few, where they simply hope to earn tax deductions, to others that have a genuine desire to do good
   (E) a variety of reasons: while some of these individuals simply hope that tax deductions will be earned, yet others have a genuine desire to do good

12. The two new <u>captains of</u> the football team,

　　　　　　A

<u>who had been chosen</u> out of over three dozen players

　　　　　　B

<u>for their</u> leadership and integrity, <u>was expected</u> to set a

C　　　　　　　　　　　　　　　　D

good example on and off the field. <u>No error</u>

　　　　　　　　　　　　　　E

13. <u>As an architect</u> and designer, Walter Gropius

　　A

<u>prioritizing</u> simplicity, clarity, <u>and sturdiness</u> in

B　　　　　　　　　　　　C

the construction <u>of office buildings</u>. <u>No error</u>

　　　　　　　D　　　　　　E

14. While <u>she was</u> growing up, Millicent <u>resented</u> her

　　　　A　　　　　　　　　　　B

younger brother's <u>habit of sneaking</u> into her room

　　　　　　　　C

<u>and reading</u> through her secret diary when she wasn't

D

at home. <u>No error</u>

　　　　E

15. <u>After much</u> deliberation, Principal Norris decided

　　A

<u>to disregard</u> the results of the student election,

　　B

<u>being caused</u> the many students who <u>had cast ballots</u>

C　　　　　　　　　　　　　D

to protest vehemently. <u>No error</u>

　　　　　　　　E

16. Every spring, the Gartners <u>spend</u> a few months in the

　　　　　　　　　　A

Catskills, <u>where</u> the entire <u>family enjoys</u> hiking,

　　　　B　　　　　　C

jogging, and <u>to watch</u> the vivid yet soothing

　　　　　D

mountain scenery. <u>No error</u>

　　　　　　E

17. In the 1992 presidential election, Bill Clinton

<u>appealed</u> to younger voters <u>by appearing</u> on the

A　　　　　　　　　　B

Arsenio Hall Show and <u>where he gave</u> a brief

　　　　　　　　C

demonstration of <u>his skills on</u> the saxophone.

　　　　　　D

<u>No error</u>

E

18. Charlotte's car <u>is just</u> as efficiently <u>engineered and</u>

　　　　A　　　　　　　B

just as aesthetically pleasing <u>than</u> Henry's, even

　　　　　　　　C

though Henry's car is much newer <u>and costs</u> almost

　　　　　　　　　　　D

fifteen thousand dollars more. <u>No error</u>

　　　　　　　　　E

19. Both of the senators from the state of Utah <u>was</u>

　　　　　　　　　　　　A

present <u>at the dedication</u> of the new highway bridge,

　　　　B

<u>which</u> was named <u>in honor</u> of a popular Salt Lake

C　　　　　　D

City industrialist. <u>No error</u>

　　　　　　　E

20. Most of the girls <u>which entered</u> the beauty pageant

　　　　　　A

<u>did so</u> because <u>they were</u> interested in earning

B　　　　　C

money to pay college tuition, <u>not because</u> they were

　　　　　　　　　D

exorbitantly proud or vain. <u>No error</u>

　　　　　　　　E

21. For every engaging and genuinely illuminating

book <u>about philosophy</u> that <u>appear</u> in print,

　　　A　　　　　　B

<u>a hundred that feature</u> inept writing and hackneyed

　　　C

concepts make their way <u>to the market</u>. <u>No error</u>

　　　　　　　　　D　　　　　E

22. <u>Without alienating</u> her peers, taking

　　A

<u>unnecessary risks</u>, or <u>compromising</u> her ethical

B　　　　　　C

standards, Olivia rose from a humble sales

representative <u>to</u> become the owner of a

　　　　　D

multimillion-dollar magazine empire. <u>No error</u>

　　　　　　　　　　　E

Practice Test 10

23. Mrs. O'Donnell and her daughter <u>were</u> at first
A

doubtful that buying a vacation house in the Poconos

<u>would be</u> a good idea, but they <u>both decided</u> to go
B   C

through with the plan after <u>her reassuring</u>
D

conversation with the realtor. <u>No error</u>
E

24. Anyone who wishes to <u>become leaders</u> should study
A

<u>classic books</u>, such as Sun Tzu's *The Art of War*,
B

<u>that describe</u> how to establish authority <u>and how to inspire</u>
C   D

respect. <u>No error</u>
E

25. I have <u>always enjoyed</u> my debates with Leo, but I
A

will also be the first <u>to admit that</u> the most recent
B

discussion between <u>he and I</u> quickly turned much
C

more aggressive <u>than I had hoped</u> it ever would.
D

<u>No error</u>
E

26. While entertaining, the glamorous new television

drama is not <u>an accurate depiction</u> of the lives
A

<u>of corporate lawyers</u>, <u>where they</u> often perform
B   C

grueling archival research and interact little

<u>with some</u> of their clients. <u>No error</u>
D   E

27. <u>With them realizing</u> that some of the residents of
A

the nursing home would be lonely <u>over the holidays</u>,
B

the <u>staff invited</u> the members of a local youth group
C

to sing songs and play charades <u>during</u> the party.
D

<u>No error</u>
E

28. <u>Taking up</u> more space than <u>any other</u> planet
A   B

<u>in our galaxy</u>, Jupiter is larger <u>than the size of</u>
C   D

Mercury, Venus, Earth, and Mars combined.

<u>No error</u>
E

29. A man accustomed to weighing <u>his</u> words calmly
A

and carefully, the French diplomat <u>decided that</u>
B

his best course of action <u>would be to</u> let the
C

Chinese ambassador and the Spanish ambassador

speak <u>for the greater</u> part of the meeting. <u>No error</u>
D   E

2

24   24   24   Unauthorized copying or   24   24   24
                                         reuse of any part of this
                                         page is illegal.

(1) There is a prized possession in my family, which has been passed down through the generations on my father's side. (2) But it isn't a typical heirloom, such as a favorite car or an old painting. (3) It is, instead, an instrument: a French horn exactly, and an instrument which brought joy and inspiration ever since my great-grandfather was alive.

(4) As far as I know, it was bought at an auction, which my great-grandfather attended right after moving to New England. (5) A proper French horn uses almost 75 feet (amazing!) of bronze tubing, though all this metal gets twisted into a compact circular shape. (6) My great-grandfather was looking for wall and over-the-fireplace decorations and the French horn looked perfect, so he purchased it for what probably wasn't a large sum and brought the horn home, where it sat unused yet winning everyone's admiration for over seventy-five years. (7) The horn eventually took hold of my father's attention. (8) He took it down and asked if anyone knew how to play it; alas, nobody did. (9) Unwilling to give up, my father bought an old yellowing manual from a secondhand store and taught himself to play; later, he joined a marching band when he entered high school. (10) Like my father, I am also interested in playing the French horn, though perhaps not in a marching band.

30. Which of the following revisions would best improve the underlined portion of sentence 3 (reproduced below)?

    It is, instead, an instrument: a French horn <u>exactly, and an instrument which brought</u> joy and inspiration ever since my great-grandfather was alive.

    (A) exactly, an instrument which has brought
    (B) exactly, an instrument continuing to bring
    (C) exactly, and this instrument will bring
    (D) exactly, which is still bringing
    (E) exactly. It brings

31. In context, which of the following revisions to sentence 4 is most needed?

    (A) Change "to New England" to "in New England".
    (B) Change "which" to "that".
    (C) Change "after" to "from".
    (D) Change "it" to "my family's French horn".
    (E) Change "it was" to "they were".

32. Which of the following revisions is most needed for the underlined portion of sentence 6 (reproduced below)?

    My great-grandfather was looking for wall and over-the-fireplace decorations and the French horn looked perfect, so he purchased it for what probably wasn't a large sum and brought the horn <u>home, where it sat unused yet winning everyone's admiration for over seventy-five years</u>.

    (A) home; and even having sat unused, it won everyone's admiration for over seventy-five years
    (B) home, in which it continued to sit unused, and continues to win everyone's admiration for over seventy-five years
    (C) home: sitting unused yet admired by everyone for over seventy-five years
    (D) home, where it sits unused but wins everyone's admiration for over seventy-five years
    (E) home. Although it sat unused, the horn would win everyone's admiration over a period of seventy-five years

33. Where in the passage would the following sentence most appropriately be inserted?

After years of staring at it, he finally saw it not as a mere decoration but as a beautiful instrument, ready to be played.

(A) At the beginning of the second paragraph
(B) Before sentence 6
(C) Immediately after sentence 7
(D) Before sentence 9
(E) After sentence 10

34. The passage would be improved by the deletion of which sentence?

(A) Sentence 2
(B) Sentence 5
(C) Sentence 6
(D) Sentence 7
(E) Sentence 9

35. Where is the most logical place to begin a new paragraph?

(A) After sentence 5
(B) After sentence 6
(C) After sentence 7
(D) After sentence 8
(E) After sentence 9

STOP
**If you finish before time is called, you may check your work on this section only.
Do not turn to any other section in the test.**

SECTION 2
Time–10 minutes
14 Questions

1. Always fascinated by the beauty and power of horses, Marcia <u>has signing up to</u> riding lessons.

   (A) has signing up to
   (B) signing up for
   (C) is signing up, and she is for
   (D) who will sign up for
   (E) has signed up for

2. Longtime fans were disappointed to find that the pop duo had changed its wardrobe, <u>its manager, and its signature musical style</u>.

   (A) its manager, and its signature musical style
   (B) its manager, and they had a signature musical style
   (C) its manager, as well as its musical style being its signature
   (D) beyond this its manager and its signature musical style being changed
   (E) its manager, and their musical style which was a signature

3. Above the rafters, <u>the spectators, cheering loudly, they filled</u> the stadium with merriment.

   (A) the spectators, cheering loudly, they filled
   (B) the spectators, cheering loudly, and filling
   (C) the spectators cheered loudly, filling
   (D) the spectators cheered loudly, they filled
   (E) the spectators cheer loudly, with filling

4. Famous for introducing great directors from abroad to American audiences, <u>Hollywood movies that he deemed poorly constructed and intellectually insulting were also attacked by film critic Roger Ebert</u>.

   (A) Hollywood movies that he deemed poorly constructed and intellectually insulting were also attacked by film critic Roger Ebert
   (B) film critic Roger Ebert attacked Hollywood movies that he deemed poorly constructed and also they were intellectually insulting
   (C) what were deemed poor construction and intellectual insults in Hollywood movies were attacked by film critic Roger Ebert
   (D) film critic Roger Ebert, attacking Hollywood movies that he deemed poorly constructed, he found them intellectually insulting
   (E) film critic Roger Ebert also attacked Hollywood movies that he deemed poorly constructed and intellectually insulting

5. Visited to this day by crowds of sightseers in Alphabet City, <u>the wooden church had once stood</u> as a testament to the encroaching gentrification of this historic urban area.

   (A) the wooden church had once stood
   (B) the wooden church stands
   (C) the wooden church has stood until recently
   (D) the wooden church while standing
   (E) stands the wooden church

6. Natural forest fires are not merely <u>destructive forces, they are instead of this a means of clearing away long-dead trees and they replenish nutrients in woodland soil</u>.

  (A) destructive forces, they are instead of this a means of clearing away long-dead trees and they replenish nutrients in woodland soil
  (B) a destructive force; such fires are a means of clearing away long-dead trees by replenishing nutrients in woodland soil
  (C) destructive forces; clearing away long-dead trees and replenishing nutrients in woodland soil are such fires and their means
  (D) destructive forces; instead, such fires are a means of clearing away long-dead trees and of replenishing nutrients in woodland soil
  (E) a destructive force, which instead of this makes them a means of clearing away long-dead trees and replenishing nutrients in woodland soil

7. <u>Although they resemble mythical sea monsters</u>, the frilled shark is not a particularly great danger to sailors and divers.

  (A) Although they resemble mythical sea monsters
  (B) Despite their resemblance to mythical sea monsters
  (C) Although it resembles a mythical sea monster
  (D) Because it resembles mythical sea monsters
  (E) As a mythical sea monster, because it resembles this

8. Yvonne found the process <u>from relocating to a new city</u> profoundly distressing, since she had not been accustomed to either fast-paced public transportation or a large variety of shops in her hometown in rural Wyoming.

  (A) from relocating to a new city
  (B) where relocation to a new city was
  (C) unlike relocation to a new city
  (D) in spite of relocation to a new city
  (E) of relocating to a new city

9. In the essay "Stranger in the Village", African-American novelist James Baldwin describes <u>the misapprehensions he encountered while visiting a small, rural community in the Swiss Alps</u>.

  (A) the misapprehensions he encountered while visiting a small, rural community in the Swiss Alps
  (B) where he encountered misapprehensions while visiting a small, rural community in the Swiss Alps
  (C) misapprehensions, in which he encountered while visiting a small, rural community in the Swiss Alps
  (D) a small, rural community in the Swiss Alps, when he encountered misapprehensions
  (E) a small, rural community in the Swiss Alps, although misapprehensions were being encountered there

10. Nicknamed the "hardest working man in show business," <u>the song "I Feel Good" is probably James Brown's most widely known recording</u>.

  (A) the song "I Feel Good" is probably James Brown's most widely known recording
  (B) James Brown's song "I Feel Good" is probably his most widely known recording
  (C) James Brown's most widely known recording is probably the song "I Feel Good"
  (D) because James Brown recorded "I Feel Good", it is probably his most widely known song
  (E) James Brown recorded "I Feel Good", which is probably his most widely known song

11. Heels were originally created to lift their wearers above dirt or garbage on the streets while <u>walking, this is why it is commonplace to see men from earlier times wearing heels too</u>.

  (A) walking, this is why it is commonplace to see men from earlier times wearing heels too
  (B) walking, and so men wearing heels is even commonplace in earlier times
  (C) walking; in earlier times, it was even commonplace to see men wearing heels
  (D) walking; resulting in the commonplace heels worn by men in earlier times
  (E) although men, walking in earlier times, commonly wore heels

205

12. While writing his script, a story about a boxer from an impoverished town in rural Mississippi, <u>the laptop unexpectedly shut down on Remy and so he lost his work</u>.

(A) the laptop unexpectedly shut down on Remy and so he lost his work
(B) Remy's laptop unexpectedly shut down and so his work was lost
(C) Remy, because the laptop shut down unexpectedly, loses his work
(D) Remy lost his work when the laptop unexpectedly shut down
(E) the laptop because of this lost Remy's work, due to an unexpected shut down

13. Unlike a parable, which is an imaginary story that sets out to teach a lesson about human conduct, <u>a tale is a story that is entertaining but that does not always contain a specific moral</u>.

(A) a tale is a story that is entertaining but that does not always contain a specific moral
(B) a tale is a story that is entertaining: but it does not always contain a specific moral
(C) a tale is an entertaining story where the moral is not always specific
(D) these stories, as tales, are entertaining despite its moral not always being specific
(E) a tale is a story that is entertaining: nonetheless, its moral not always being specific

14. A wiki is an online page or document that can be edited by any of its <u>visitors, not only an editor who possesses extensive knowledge of the topics covered and a non-specialist who is casually browsing the Internet</u>.

(A) visitors, not only an editor who possesses extensive knowledge of the topics covered and a non-specialist who is casually browsing the Internet
(B) visitors, perhaps being an editor who possesses extensive knowledge of the topics covered and a non-specialist who is casually browsing the Internet
(C) visitors, such as an editor who possesses extensive knowledge of the topics covered, but also a non-specialist who is casually browsing the Internet
(D) visitors, neither an editor who possesses extensive knowledge of the topics covered nor non-specialists, who are casual and also browse the Internet
(E) visitors, from an editor who possesses extensive knowledge of the topics covered to a non-specialist who is casually browsing the Internet

STOP
**If you finish before time is called, you may check your work on this section only.
Do not turn to any other section in the test.**

Chapter 25

ANSWER KEY

2⃞ 25   25   25   25   25   25

Unauthorized copying or reuse of any part of this page is illegal.

Answer Key

PRACTICE TEST 1

Section 1

1.	B	13.	D	25.	C
2.	D	14.	A	26.	B
3.	E	15.	E	27.	C
4.	C	16.	A	28.	A
5.	B	17.	B	29.	D
6.	E	18.	D	30.	C
7.	A	19.	C	31.	B
8.	E	20.	D	32.	A
9.	C	21.	D	33.	B
10.	B	22.	A	34.	D
11.	E	23.	D	35.	D
12.	C	24.	B		

Section 2

1.	D	6.	E	11.	A
2.	C	7.	D	12.	D
3.	B	8.	A	13.	A
4.	E	9.	E	14.	E
5.	C	10.	D		

PRACTICE TEST 2

Section 1

1.	C	13.	B	25.	A
2.	B	14.	D	26.	E
3.	C	15.	C	27.	D
4.	E	16.	C	28.	E
5.	D	17.	D	29.	D
6.	B	18.	C	30.	B
7.	A	19.	A	31.	A
8.	B	20.	A	32.	E
9.	D	21.	C	33.	C
10.	E	22.	B	34.	B
11.	B	23.	D	35.	D
12.	B	24.	E		

Section 2

1.	C	6.	B	11.	E
2.	B	7.	D	12.	A
3.	C	8.	D	13.	E
4.	B	9.	C	14.	C
5.	E	10.	A		

PRACTICE TEST 3

Section 1

1.	A	13.	C	25.	B
2.	C	14.	C	26.	D
3.	C	15.	D	27.	D
4.	A	16.	B	28.	E
5.	B	17.	E	29.	A
6.	A	18.	C	30.	A
7.	E	19.	C	31.	C
8.	D	20.	E	32.	B
9.	D	21.	A	33.	E
10.	B	22.	B	34.	D
11.	A	23.	C	35.	C
12.	C	24.	B		

Section 2

1.	C	6.	C	11.	D
2.	B	7.	D	12.	C
3.	C	8.	A	13.	C
4.	B	9.	B	14.	E
5.	D	10.	E		

PRACTICE TEST 4

Section 1

1.	B	13.	A	25.	D
2.	B	14.	C	26.	C
3.	C	15.	C	27.	B
4.	D	16.	A	28.	B
5.	E	17.	C	29.	C
6.	E	18.	B	30.	C
7.	D	19.	A	31.	B
8.	C	20.	D	32.	D
9.	C	21.	A	33.	D
10.	B	22.	B	34.	E
11.	D	23.	A	35.	D
12.	A	24.	A		

Section 2

1.	E	6.	D	11.	C
2.	B	7.	B	12.	A
3.	A	8.	E	13.	B
4.	C	9.	E	14.	C
5.	B	10.	B		

Answer Key

PRACTICE TEST 5

Section 1

1.	B	13.	B	25.	C
2.	B	14.	B	26.	A
3.	C	15.	C	27.	B
4.	E	16.	C	28.	B
5.	A	17.	D	29.	C
6.	D	18.	A	30.	A
7.	C	19.	A	31.	E
8.	C	20.	D	32.	E
9.	B	21.	B	33.	C
10.	B	22.	D	34.	D
11.	C	23.	C	35.	A
12.	D	24.	A		

Section 2

1.	E	6.	D	11.	E
2.	B	7.	D	12.	B
3.	E	8.	B	13.	C
4.	C	9.	E	14.	E
5.	B	10.	C		

PRACTICE TEST 7

Section 1

1.	A	13.	D	25.	C
2.	C	14.	C	26.	B
3.	B	15.	C	27.	C
4.	E	16.	C	28.	A
5.	E	17.	D	29.	E
6.	C	18.	E	30.	E
7.	C	19.	D	31.	A
8.	B	20.	C	32.	B
9.	D	21.	A	33.	B
10.	D	22.	D	34.	A
11.	C	23.	E	35.	E
12.	D	24.	C		

Section 2

1.	E	6.	E	11.	E
2.	C	7.	C	12.	E
3.	B	8.	B	13.	C
4.	D	9.	C	14.	B
5.	A	10.	D		

PRACTICE TEST 6

Section 1

1.	C	13.	A	25.	C
2.	A	14.	C	26.	E
3.	E	15.	B	27.	B
4.	C	16.	A	28.	D
5.	B	17.	E	29.	B
6.	E	18.	C	30.	E
7.	B	19.	A	31.	A
8.	D	20.	B	32.	D
9.	E	21.	B	33.	B
10.	A	22.	C	34.	A
11.	C	23.	C	35.	B
12.	B	24.	D		

Section 2

1.	E	6.	C	11.	C
2.	C	7.	A	12.	E
3.	A	8.	B	13.	D
4.	B	9.	B	14.	B
5.	E	10.	B		

PRACTICE TEST 8

Section 1

1.	C	13.	A	25.	D
2.	B	14.	C	26.	D
3.	E	15.	D	27.	E
4.	C	16.	C	28.	B
5.	D	17.	A	29.	C
6.	B	18.	D	30.	E
7.	A	19.	C	31.	A
8.	E	20.	D	32.	B
9.	C	21.	D	33.	A
10.	B	22.	D	34.	D
11.	E	23.	E	35.	E
12.	B	24.	D		

Section 2

1.	B	6.	C	11.	C
2.	C	7.	B	12.	B
3.	D	8.	C	13.	B
4.	D	9.	B	14.	D
5.	E	10.	E		

Answer Key

PRACTICE TEST 9

Section 1

1.	E	13.	A	25.	C
2.	E	14.	B	26.	C
3.	C	15.	D	27.	D
4.	B	16.	B	28.	A
5.	A	17.	A	29.	A
6.	C	18.	C	30.	A
7.	D	19.	B	31.	E
8.	B	20.	C	32.	C
9.	C	21.	D	33.	B
10.	B	22.	D	34.	C
11.	C	23.	B	35.	E
12.	D	24.	D		

Section 2

1.	A	6.	E	11.	D
2.	A	7.	A	12.	B
3.	E	8.	C	13.	C
4.	D	9.	B	14.	C
5.	B	10.	B		

PRACTICE TEST 10

Section 1

1.	E	13.	B	25.	C
2.	C	14.	E	26.	C
3.	B	15.	C	27.	A
4.	D	16.	D	28.	D
5.	C	17.	C	29.	E
6.	A	18.	C	30.	A
7.	B	19.	A	31.	D
8.	B	20.	A	32.	E
9.	E	21.	B	33.	C
10.	D	22.	E	34.	B
11.	C	23.	D	35.	B
12.	D	24.	A		

Section 2

1.	E	6.	D	11.	C
2.	A	7.	C	12.	D
3.	C	8.	E	13.	A
4.	E	9.	A	14.	E
5.	B	10.	E		

CPSIA information can be obtained at www.ICGtesting.com
Printed in the USA
LVOW09s1511101214

418172LV00013B/530/P